JRE STUDIES IN RELIGIOUS ETHICS II

EDITOR	James Childress	*Kennedy Institute of Ethics, Georgetown University*
ASSOCIATE EDITORS:	Margaret Farley	*Yale University*
	Douglas Sturm	*Bucknell University*
	Stanley Hauerwas	*University of Notre Dame*
	David Wills	*Amherst College*

GENERAL EDITOR,   JRE Publications:

	Charles Reynolds	*University of Tennessee*

Studies in Religious Ethics is an extension of THE JOURNAL OF RELIGIOUS ETHICS and sponsored by The University of Tennessee and The Kennedy Institute of Ethics.

JRE STUDIES IN RELIGIOUS ETHICS I: *LOVE AND SOCIETY: ESSAYS IN THE ETHICS OF PAUL RAMSEY.* Edited by James Johnson and David Smith.

JRE STUDIES IN RELIGIOUS ETHICS II: *ABORTION AND THE ROMAN CATHOLIC CHURCH.* By Susan Teft Nicholson.

ABORTION AND THE ROMAN CATHOLIC CHURCH

by

Susan T. Nicholson

Published by

Religious Ethics, Inc.

Distributed By
JRE
Department of Religious Studies
University of Tennessee
Knoxville, Tennessee 37916

Library of Congress Cataloging in Publication Data
Nicholson, Susan T.
  Abortion and the Roman Catholic Church.

  (JRE studies in religious ethics : no. 2)
  1. Abortion—Religious Aspects. I. Title.
II. Series
HQ767.3.N5   261.83   SF77-405
ISBN 0-931886-00-7
ISSN 0145-2797

Printed in the United States of America

Holston Printing Company, Inc.
Knoxville, Tennessee 37919

Contents

iv

CHAPTER III.
Grisez's Revision of The Double Effect Principle 41

CHAPTER IV.
Abortion Following Rape: Thomson's Defense of Abortion 49

CHAPTER VI.
Abortion on Fetal Indications 79

CHAPTER VII.

Prepared with the assistance of Glenn Graber.

Preface

The practice of abortion is apt to trigger deep and powerful emotions not only in the pregnant woman and those performing the abortion but also among others not so directly involved. Moreover, it touches diverse, changing, and often conflicting interests. The interest of the mother, to have the right to decide on the course of the pregnancy, can come into conflict with the interest of the father, to have at least a say in that decision, with that of society at large which may act as the representative of the future citizen and the guardian of the size of the population when individual reproductive intitiative results in seriously disruptive trends, and finally with that of the medical profession which is charged with the task of carrying out abortion decisions and of coping with their medical consequences.

It is plain that changes of various kinds adversely affect these interest groups and so give rise to demands for modifications of social and legislative policies which would protect these interests. I have in mind changes such as medical advances (say, the invention of antiseptic techniques which make abortions safe, or of a simple abortive pill which would enable a woman to terminate her unwanted pregnancy in complete secrecy), or changes in population trends (as, for instance, in Romania where a serious decline in the birth rate was followed by restrictive legislation on abortion), or changes in political conditions (as, for instance, in Japan where the termination of the expansionistic policy after Japan's defeat in World War II and the consequent loss of territory suitable for settling the increasing numbers forced the Japanese government to stop population growth by all available means including abortion).

During the last 20 years, such modifications in social and legislative policy on abortion have taken place in country after country, most recently also in the United States, where the Supreme Court passed a landmark decision on state abortion laws (Roe v. Wade, 1973). The Court found that a pregnant woman had a constitutional right to an abortion whenever continued pregnancy would endanger her health, and that during the first trimester of the pregnancy she even had the right to terminate her pregnancy for any reasons whatever. There can be no doubt that this decision is widely felt to be of profound significance for the lives of many women and through its far-reaching effects also for the lives of all of us.

Such radical changes sometimes evoke strong reactions. It is not unlikely that we shall in the near future witness such reactions also in this country. As I write these lines, strong efforts are being made to insert into the presidential election campaign the issue of a constitutional amendment on abortion. The chances therefore are that, in this country at any rate, citizens will have an opportunity in one way or another to have some say on what shall be the law on abortions. This gives them a special interest and an obligation to acquaint themselves with the complex issues on which they may have to cast their votes.

This admirable book provides reliable guidance on one extremely important, perhaps the most important, aspect of this multi-faceted problem. It deals in considerable depth with the central moral issue: is it ever morally right for a woman to have an abortion and, if so, in what circumstances? This is surely the fundamental question on which most others turn. It may be a consideration against prohibiting abortion that such a prohibition in some sense favors the rich because they can afford to travel to other countries or states where abortion is permissible, while the poor have to resort to the back-door abortionists and risk their health or even lives in doing so. But such considerations presuppose that it is not wrong for the state to make abortion lawful, for presumably no one would wish to argue that abortion should become lawful even if it is wrong to make it so. No one would wish to argue that laws prohibiting murder should be abolished because in a similar way they favor the rich who can afford to hire experts to kill their enemies, or lawyers to get them off. The question whether abortion should continue or cease to be lawful hinges primarily on the question of whether abortion itself is wrong. Even if abortion continues to be lawful, pregnant women and their physicians should not, as moral beings, simply avail themselves of that legal license to suit their personal convenience or interest, but should base their decision to abort or not to abort on the answer to that fundamental moral question. And if abortion is made unlawful, then similarly each person should base on that same answer his or her decision whether to support or fight the new law.

Dr. Nicholson conducts her examination within a framework which is interesting on its own account and which enables her to present the intricate problems with great simplicity and lucidity. She sets out from what is undoubtedly the most uncompromising condemnation of abortion, the argument of the Roman Catholic Church, noting its great strengths and probing for weaknesses. The Catholic argument is an eminently suitable starting point, because it is by common consent the most fully worked out and most carefully reasoned case on the problem of abortion and because, most importantly, its appeal is not narrow or sectarian, but purports to rest on the common moral convictions of this pluralistic society, and so must, if sound, be accepted by everybody, whether Catholic or not.

From a brief but fascinating and, it seems to me, accurate and fair review of the history of the Catholic position, she extracts the two major grounds on which the Catholic condemnation of abortion rests. The first derives from the hostile Catholic stance (though it is by no means peculiar to it) on sexual activity and pleasure. With minor fluctuations, that stance has remained unchanged throughout the Church's history, though she notes a certain mellowing during the last 50 years. The central tenet is that sexual activity involves a type of immoral pleasure which can be redeemed only by its subordination to reproduction. Even this is possible only because reproduction depends on sexual intercourse and sexual intercourse involves that immoral pleasure. If reproduction could be divorced from sexual activity, as in virgin birth, sexual activity and its allied pleasures would lack all moral justification. On the older view, exemplified by St. Augustine, the pleasure is morally permissible only if it is merely acquiesced in as a virtually unavoidable by-product of procreation. On the newer view, exemplified by Pope Paul VI's "Humanae Vitae" (1968), the pleasure may be welcomed as an expression of mutual love (the unitive as opposed to the procreative function of sexual activity), provided the procreative function is not frustrated by artificial contraceptive devices. On such a view, a decision to abort must be read as expressing an immoral attitude towards sexual activity, since it violates the requirement that at least one of the purposes of such activity must be procreation. Nicholson does not probe this line of argument because it rests on a moral premise, the tying of sexual activity to reproduction, which is not now, if indeed it ever was, an element in the common moral convictions of our society. She merely allows herself the speculation that for many people part of the appeal of the Catholic case against abortion may be anchored in their own puritanical attitude towards sexual pleasure.

Her main effort, however, is devoted to the second line of argument which really can claim to rest on a universally accepted moral principle, the sanctity of human life. The argument starts from the premise that a human fetus, throughout all the stages of its prenatal existence, is an innocent human being. And it concludes from this that all intentional abortion is the intentional killing of an innocent human being, and therefore morally indefensible. Two main doubts naturally arise. Is a fetus at every or any stage a human being, in the sense of a person, or at any rate a being to whom we must ascribe a right to life? And, supposing that the fetus really is a human being, is it always morally wrong intentionally to kill a human being?

Most writers on the subject have wearied themselves and their readers by trying to answer the first question, but no one has so far come up with a cogent argument for picking one stage rather than another as the point at which human life in the crucial sense begins. (Even Catholic writers have not always held that it begins at conception.) Nicholson wisely does not travel that well-worn track to nowhere. Instead, she simply adopts, for the purpose of her argument, the supposition that the fetus is at all stages an innocent human being, and concentrates on the second question, that is, which, if any, abortions would be morally permissible, should that supposition be true.

Some readers may perhaps deplore her failure to deal with the first question which usually occupies pride of place in treatises on abortion. And it must be admitted that her strategy leaves unanswered an important question, one we can hardly ignore when we are making our judgment on abortion. For if the supposition is false, if the fetus is at no stage or only at later stages a human being in the relevant sense, then the Catholic argument from the wrongness of killing innocent human beings loses at least some of its bite. However, given our present inadequate understanding of the nature of personhood, and of the grounds for ascribing to a being the right to life, discussions of this problem must inevitably remain inconclusive and so incapable of providing objective guidance. I therefore think the author has chosen wisely in not making yet another attempt to tell us where human life in the crucial sense begins, particularly in view of the fact that she has so much to tell us that is conclusive and practically helpful on the second question.

It would be inappropriate for me here in this Preface to anticipate Dr. Nicholson's answers to that question, but perhaps I may mention one especially helpful and illuminating point in her argument. Obviously, how we must judge a pregnant woman's decision to terminate her unwanted pregnancy will depend on precisely how we should construe the relation between her and her fetus. If we conceive of it as a relation between two physically independent persons, we shall find comparatively few circumstances in which an abortion decision is morally justifiable. But must we, or indeed can we, look at it in this way? Nicholson characterizes the relationship quite differently. In virtue of the pregnancy, the mother's body provides, sometimes to her detriment, occasionally at the cost of her life, the necessary life support for the growing fetus. If we accept this characterization of the relationship, and I can see no good reason for rejecting it, then abortion is the termination of such life support. But that seems a very different matter, morally speaking, from the killing of a physically independent person. It is not nearly as obvious that a person must in all circumstances and at all costs continue to give another person life support as that he must not kill him.

In any case, whether in the end a reader accepts or rejects her conclusions, he or she will certainly emerge from the experience with a deepened understanding of the strengths and weaknesses of what is rightly regarded as the strongest case against abortion, and so with a deepened understanding of the problem itself.

Kurt Baier
University of Pittsburgh

Acknowledgments

I wish to thank Marilyn Frye, who patiently read and criticized numerous drafts of chapters IV-VI; Kurt Baier, who directed the dissertation upon which this is based; and my parents, Frank and Agnes Nicholson, who encouraged me throughout.

Among the many other persons offering personal support and/or assistance with the manuscript, I am especially grateful to Willard Arnett, Ruth Barron, Nancy Crumbine, Janelle and Martin Greenberg, Sandra Guzzy, André Hellegers, Peter Safar, Deborah Sagar, Thomas Schwartz, and Joan Straumanis.

I appreciate the opportunity provided by the Society for Women in Philosophy to present a version of chapter II.

Finally, I am grateful to the American Council of Learned Societies, and to Chatham College, for grants which enabled me to complete my research.

Chatham College

TO

Charlotte Andrews

CHAPTER I

The Twofold Basis of the Roman Catholic Condemnation of Abortion

1. On January 22, 1973, the Supreme Court of the United States brought to a close a brief period of intense controversy by declaring it a constitutionally protected right to kill an organism whose destruction, only six years earlier, had been a felony in each of the fifty states (*Roe v. Wade*, 410 US 113, 1973). The Court divided the period of pregnancy into trimesters, and held the following:

(1) During the first trimester, the abortion decision *must* be left to the medical judgment of the pregnant woman's physician.
(2) During and subsequent to the second trimester, the state *may*, if it wishes, regulate abortion in ways reasonably related to the preservation and protection of maternal health.
(3) During the third trimester, the state *may*, if it wishes, regulate or even prohibit abortion in order to promote its interest in potential human life, *except* where abortion is necessary for the preservation of the life or health of the mother. The third trimester was said to begin at viability, that is, the point at which the fetus is able to live outside the mother's uterus, albeit with artificial aid.

In its decision, the Court thus forbade the state to pass legislation aimed at protecting the life of a non-viable fetus, and permitted but did not require that legislation be passed to protect a viable one. Furthermore, the notion of health relied upon by the Court included all factors—physical, emotional, psychological, and familial—relevant to the woman's well-being.[1] It would appear that on this broad understanding of health, any woman who strongly desired to abort her viable fetus could make a persuasive argument that abortion was necessary to preserve her health. The decision invalidated the laws of all fifty states, including those with recently passed "abortion-on-request" legislation.

This decision, acclaimed by some as a vindication of individual freedom in a pluralistic society, was deplored by others as an exercise in raw judicial power marking the end of the Judaeo-Christian era in law and the beginning of a new era guided by considerations of quality rather than equality of lives. Human Life Amendments were introduced in Congress with the expressed aim of returning the nation to its 200-year-old commitment to what some referred to as the centerpiece of Anglo-American law, namely, the inviolability of the life of every innocent human being. Although leaders of the Roman Catholic Church were conspicuous among the critics of the decision, they were careful to reject the suggestion that they were attempting to impose their morality on others. "While we are leaders of the Catholic Church in the United States," one said, "we believe that what we say expresses the convictions of many Americans who are members of other faiths and of no faith" (*Documentation on the Right to Life and Abortion*, 1974:36).

This study is an assessment of the Roman Catholic claim that Catholic doctrine on abortion articulates values common to most members of this Judaeo-Christian society—values, moreover, which are properly enforced by law in a pluralistic society. At issue is whether or not a common commitment to the sanctity of human life, together with acceptance of the claim that the fetus is a human being, renders a condemnation of abortion inescapable. That the fetus is a human being will be assumed for the sake of argument, throughout the study. The study focuses on Roman Catholic doctrine, since it is the source of the most influential and rigorously developed arguments against abortion.

To characterize a particular view on abortion as "the" Roman Catholic doctrine, does not imply unanimity among Catholics with regard to abortion. While the condemnation of abortion from conception onwards is characterized in the most authoritative documents of the Church as "ever unchanged and immutable" (Paul VI, 1972:333) and "the constant teaching of the supreme doctrinal authority" ("Declaration on Abortion," 1974:251), there are Roman Catholic theologians who do dissent, in part, from this teaching. Their dissent will be noted where appropriate. Nevertheless, it is the orthodox Roman Catholic doctrine, and not dissenting Catholic opinion, which is the subject of this study. That doctrine is expressed in broad outline in papal addresses, declarations of the Roman Curia,[2] and pronouncements of the Second Vatican Council,[3] and is elaborated in a remarkably consistent fashion in a number of Roman Catholic moral theology texts. The orthodox doctrine, moreover, is vigorously defended by the Roman Catholic hierarchy in the United States, under whose powerful influence it has been invoked on behalf of a constitutional amendment to forbid the taking of fetal life from conception onwards. Thus, it is the orthodox doctrine which plays a central role in the present public debate on abortion.

This chapter sets out, in a general way, the grounds for the Roman Catholic condemnation of abortion, and formulates the main questions to be treated in subsequent chapters.

I. Abortion as a Sin of Sex

2. The Roman Catholic condemnation of abortion is complex in that typically it has two sources: (1) an ethic of sex, and (2) an ethic of killing. For reasons to be explained subsequently, this study focuses on abortion as it relates to the Catholic ethic of killing. Nevertheless, it is instructive to identify those aspects of Catholic sexual doctrine which are relevant to abortion.

Many non-Catholics and Catholics alike associate abortion with non-marital sexual relations. Women who abort are frequently perceived as destroying evidence of and evading responsibility for their non-marital sexual activity. Correlatively, restrictive abortion laws are urged as a deterrent to, or punishment for, such supposed sexual immorality. A standard rebuttal of this position consists in pointing out that a large percentage of women who abort have conceived as a result of marital sex.

It perhaps is not generally recognized that this rebuttal does not touch the singularly Roman Catholic association of abortion with sexual sin. Throughout its history, Roman Church leadership has sought to maintain, in one form or another, a link between sexual activity and procreation.[4] In its present form, church doctrine forbids the separation of the unitive (love-fostering) aspect of sexuality from the procreative aspect. This principle underlies the papal reaffirmation of the immorality of artificial birth control (Paul VI, 1968), and by it, all abortion stands equally condemned. Abortion deliberately deprives a preceding sexual act of its procreative aspect while leaving its unitive aspect intact. Abortion, thus, is held to be wrong, and the marital status of the sexual couple is irrelevant to this species of sexual sin.

It follows that even if the fetus were not a human being, Catholics would still view abortion as evil. This explains why the condemnation of abortion did not falter during those periods when Church fathers rejected the notion that a human being was present from conception onwards.

Catholic insistence on the procreative function of sexuality is sometimes believed to arise from a desire for a high Catholic birth rate. This interpretation is inconsistent, however, with the superior position accorded virginity in Catholic doctrine. In the medieval period, some theologians accorded special honor to the virginity or complete sexual abstinence even of married couples (Noonan, 1966:70, 277-78).

I suggest that the emphasis upon the procreative aspect of sexuality reflects instead a hostility towards sexual pleasure. For all but the last hundred years of the Church's history, theologians generally considered it at least venial, and perhaps mortal sin, to engage in sexual relations for the purpose of experiencing sexual pleasure. By insisting that sex be procreative, Catholic moralists were able to limit sharply the extent and variety of sexual pleasure, and to "excuse" what pleasure remained by reference to the child-rearing services the sexual couple rendered the species.

One effect of this theological *animus* towards sexual pleasure was the elimination of any basis for a connection between sexual pleasure and the expression of love. If one cannot legitimately seek sensuous pleasure in sexual experience, then the arousal and gratification of sensuous desires cannot be an embodiment of a virtuous love. Thus while love was a vaunted Christian virtue, and although marital love was required of those engaging in sexual acts, the obedient Catholic couple was one who in an important sense experienced *sex without love.*

This stunning impoverishment of life was imposed upon Catholics by exclusively male and predominantly celibate theologians for almost 19 centuries. It was not, in fact, until 1852 that a Catholic theologian, Gury, thought to suggest that a legitimate function of marital sex might be the promotion of love (Noonan, 1966:491-92). As noted, present Church doctrine gives equal weight to the unitive and procreative aspects of marital sex. In refusing to grant complete independence to the unitive aspect, however, the Catholic Church is still captive to its traditional antipathy to erotic love. A brief historical sketch will illustrate the role of this antipathy in the Roman Catholic condemnation of abortion.

3. Early Church theologians taught that intercourse was immoral unless engaged in for the purpose of procreation. According to Noonan (1966:46-49) this rule, lacking any explicit Biblical basis, was borrowed from the teaching of the Roman Stoics, Musonius Rufus and Seneca. This places the intellectual heritage of the Catholic sexual ethic in a philosophical movement whose adherents sought to make themselves invulnerable to misfortune by freeing themselves of attachment to whatever was not under their control. A "tranquil flow of life" was thus achieved at the cost of a deadening of affect in certain areas. This theme is apparent in the works of the two best known Roman Stoics, Epictetus (c. 50 A.D.-c. 130 A.D.) and Marcus Aurelius (121 A.D.-180 A.D.).

Epictetus taught that one who would be free must learn to desire only what was totally within one's power. Marcus Aurelius strove for equanimity by observing that no matter what men might do to him, they could not alter the justice, purity, wisdom and sobriety of his mind. Attaching value only to what was thus completely subject to his control, Marcus Aurelius was led to an affirmation of the Socratic view that it is not within the power of an evil man to harm a good one.

Like the *Apology* (28d-30a, 41d) in which Socrates makes this surprising claim,[5] Marcus Aurelius' *Meditations* is pervaded by a strong sense of impending death. Death is of course the final misfortune, and the dissolution of the body in death is undeniable. From a psychological point of view, both the trilogy relating the trial and death of Socrates and *Meditations* give the impression that the authors have reacted to the agonizing brevity of bodily existence by denying themselves the experience of human goods in which the body plays a conspicuous role. Socrates is never more lyrical in describing the philosophical flight from the body, nor more vivid in portraying the manner in which bodily pleasures imprison the soul, than in the dialogue which takes place on the day he knows he is to die.[6]

I am suggesting that the restrictive Roman Catholic sexual ethic might plausibly be viewed as originating in a self-protective withdrawal from whatever is subject to loss. Sexual pleasures are especially to be abjured, as they are capable of evoking the most intense attachment to the body and to another human being, neither of which is totally within one's control. Pleasure in sexual experience must consequently be extirpated, or at least strictly curtailed. Faced with inevitable human loss, a most stringent prophylactic is proposed: anticipate that loss by a self-imposed deprivation.

It is Noonan's view that the rule of procreative intent arose and was reaffirmed in early Christianity partially in reaction to two rival religious movements—Gnosticism and Manicheanism—which rigorously condemned procreation. Both the Gnostics and the Manichees were suspected by the orthodox Christian of assigning non-procreative sexual activity a central place in their religious rites. It was believed, for example, that the Gnostics engaged in ritual meals of human semen and menses, the semen having been procured by *coitus interruptus*, masturbation, or homosexual acts (Noonan, 1966:95). A reaction to Manichean doctrine would appear to be especially likely in the case of St. Augustine, who had himself been an earlier devotee of the Manichean movement.

4. Whatever its origins, insistence on a subjective procreative intent in sexual activity was incorporated into the teaching of St. Augustine (354-430), where it was to exercise a dominant influence on the Church for the next ten centuries. (See, for example, *The Good of Marriage*, ch. 6.) Adoption of the procreative requirement as formulated by Augustine implies the immorality of the following:

(1) sexual acts other than intercourse,
(2) intercourse which was believed to be, or was deliberately made to be, incapable of procreation,
(3) intercourse which was believed to be capable of procreation but which was not performed solely for that purpose.[7]

The first category includes all sexual activity between persons of the same sex, heterosexual activity such as anal or oral sex, and *coitus interruptus*. The second category includes intercourse with a person believed to be sterile, as well as intercourse during what was erroneously believed to be a monthly sterile period in women. It also includes the use of whatever was believed to have contraceptive properties, such as herbal potions and salves.

It is evident that Augustine's teaching originated in an aversion to sexual pleasure rather than in a concern that there be more births. In fact, he was indifferent even to the survival of the species. In a work in which he encouraged continence both without and within marriage, he raised the rhetorical question: "What if all men should be willing to restrain themselves from all intercourse, how would the human race survive?" Augustine (*The Good of Marriage*, ch. 10) answered easily, "Would that all men had this wish. . . . Much more quickly would the City of God be filled and the end of time be hastened."

Augustine gave a Christian perspective to the earlier pagan denigration of sexual desires by explaining "concupiscence" as an effect of the original sin inherited by the descendents of Adam (Noonan, 1966:133-34). Augustine's contempt for sex nourished, or was nourished by, his low regard for women. "I feel," he wrote, "that nothing more turns the masculine mind from the heights than female blandishments and that contact of bodies without which a wife may not be had" (Quoted in Noonan, 1966:126). And while admitting that women were useful in generating, Augustine could not see what help a woman would be to a man apart from that (Noonan, 1977:129).

The following passage from Augustine's *Marriage and Concupiscence* is particularly relevant to our discussion.

> It is one thing not to lie except with the sole will of generating: this has no fault. It is another to seek the pleasure of the flesh in lying, although within the limits of marriage: this has venial fault. I am supposing that then, although you are not lying for the sake of procreating offspring, you are not for the sake of lust obstructing their procreation by an evil prayer or an evil deed. Those who do this, although they are called husband and wife, are not; nor do they retain any reality of marriage, but with a respectable name cover a shame. They give themselves away, indeed, when they go so far as to expose the children who are born to them against their will; for they hate to nourish or to have those whom they feared to bear. Therefore a dark iniquity rages against those whom they unwillingly have borne, and with open iniquity this comes to light; a hidden shame is demonstrated by manifest cruelty. Sometimes this lustful cruelty, or cruel lust, comes to this, that they even procure poisons of sterility and, if these do not work, extinguish and destroy the fetus in some way in the womb, preferring that their offspring die before it lives, or if it was already alive in the womb to kill it before it was born. Assuredly if both husband and wife are like this, they are not married, and if they were like this from the beginning they come together not joined in matrimony but in seduction. If both are not like this, I dare to say that either the wife is in a fashion the harlot of her husband or he is an adulterer with his own wife. (Quoted in Noonan, 1966:136)

Two points bear noting. (1) Augustine moves easily from a condemnation of attempts to obstruct procreation to a condemnation of abortion and infanticide. Each violates the requirement of a procreative intent in intercourse stated at the beginning of the passage.[8] (2) Augustine shows a willingness to add to the moral force of his condemnation by using terms which, properly speaking, are inapplicable. For a man to be an adulterer with his own wife is, strictly speaking, an impossibility. Other early churchmen, in a similar inflation of moral rhetoric, branded persons using contraceptive potions, men who had castrated themselves, and even homosexuals as "parricides" and "murderers" (Noonan, 1966:91, 95, 100). That the latter terms were so loosely used should be kept in mind when assessing the Roman Catholic claim that the Church has always opposed abortion as a sin of killing.

Beginning with the words "Sometimes this lustful cruelty," the passage was incorporated into the *Decretum* compiled by Gratian in 1140. The *Decretum* was treated as part of the basic law of the Roman Catholic Church until the enactment of the new *Code of Canon Law* in 1917. It was also incorporated into Peter Lombard's *Sentences*, a theological text of signal influence. Thus, in what Noonan (1966:174) calls the most important teaching on contraception in the Middle Ages, abortion is discussed together with contraception as *sexual* sin.

5. Another classical text linking abortion and contraception was contributed by a bishop committed to the Augustinian doctrine that a procreative intent is morally required for intercourse. A letter written by Caesarius, a 6th century bishop of Arles, contains a condemnation of abortion as homicide, followed by these words:

> Who is he who cannot warn that no woman may take a potion so that she is unable to conceive or condemns in herself the nature which God willed to be fecund. As often as she could have conceived or given birth, *of that many homicides she will be held guilty*, and, unless she undergoes suitable penance, she will be damned by eternal death in hell. If a woman does not wish to have children, let her enter into a religious agreement with her husband; for chastity is the sole sterility of a Christian woman. (Quoted in Noonan, 1966:146, italics added)

The force of the condemnation of abortion as a sin of killing is completely undercut by Caesarius' subsequent treatment of the use of contraceptive potions as homicide.[9] The last sentence in this passage suggests that the sin which is uppermost in the author's mind is not that of killing an innocent human being, but that of having sexual intercourse without the desire of procreating. Again, a term applicable to killing is wrenched from its proper context to impress upon the reader the true gravity of non-procreative sex.

The following text, repeating the teaching of Caesarius, appears in the 11th century *Decretum* of Buchard.

> If someone to satisfy his lust or in deliberate hatred does something to a man or woman so that no children be born of him or her, or gives them to drink, so that he cannot generate or she conceive, let it be held as homicide. (Quoted in Noonan, 1966:168)

This text became canon law in the 13th century, and was also preserved in the law of the Catholic Church until 1917. Although it treats both abortion and the use of contraceptive potions as homicide, it is again clear that the sin which links the two is really lust.

6. By the 12th century, Augustine's doctrine of procreative intent was well established. There were, however, mild dissents.

A minority of theologians maintained that intercourse might also be initiated for the purpose of avoiding extramarital sex. Although this view conflicted with Augustine's, it did not displace procreation as the sole positive value of sexual activity.

Another dispute developed over whether the seeking of pleasure in intercourse was venial sin, as Augustine had taught, or mortal sin. Some theologians holding the more severe view that the seeking of pleasure was mortal sin also believed that the mere *experiencing* of sexual pleasure during intercourse was a venial sin.

Two popes held this belief: Pope Gregory the Great (in office at the turn of the seventh century), and the 13th century Pope Innocent III. Innocent III queried, "Who does not know that conjugal intercourse is never committed without itching of the flesh, and heat and foul concupiscence, whence the conceived seeds are befouled and corrupted?" (Quoted in Noonan, 1966:197). To Gregory, it was a miracle if, even with a procreative intent, one could manage to have intercourse without sin. Responding to this problem, William of Auxerre, writing at the beginning of the 16th century, was driven to propose a highly refined distinction between enjoying and suffering sexual pleasure, only the latter being free from sin.

7. In the 13th century, St. Thomas Aquinas accepted Augustine's requirement of procreative intent, his synthesis of original sin and sex, and his low opinion of women. In Aquinas' teaching, however, the objective rather than subjective aspect of sexual acts is prominent.

The basic Thomist assumption is that sexual acts are "by nature" ordained towards procreation. Acts which violate this natural order are injuries against God, and as such occupy the supreme position in Thomas' hierarchy of sexual sin. As a criterion of "natural," Thomas adopted the depositing of semen in the "fit vessel" (Noonan, 1966:225). Thomas (*ST* 2-2, Q. 154, Art. 12) does not shrink from drawing the conclusion that rape (in which semen is properly deposited) is a lesser sin than "unnatural" sex with one's spouse.

On Thomas' view, neither intercourse with a sterile partner nor the use of contraceptive potions was unnatural. Although both were wrong on the Augustinian view adopted by Thomas, neither impeded the depositing of semen in the vagina. Thus, one could engage in a particular sexual act which precluded procreation without sinning against nature. This, of course, does not mean that Thomas' notion of what was natural was unrelated to what was procreative. Intercourse is the only sexual act from which procreation can result.

Thomas (*ST* 2-2, Q. 153, Art. 2) argued that the preservation of the species requires that sexual acts be directed to generation. So rational a man as he, however, must have been aware that species survival does not require that no unnatural sexual activity occur, but only that some natural activity occur. Furthermore, that Thomas was not unduly worried about the preservation of the species is evident from his preference for virginity, and for complete sexual abstinence even among the married.

8. During the period 1450-1750 the Augustinian doctrine was somewhat weakened. The non-procreative purpose of avoiding fornication was accepted as a lawful one for initiating intercourse. In addition, several major theologians defended the view that to seek pleasure in marital intercourse was

licit. This view, however, failed to gain majority support. Furthermore, its promoters made no mention of a connection between sexual pleasure and the expression of love.

Sanchez, a 17th century Jesuit moralist who specialized in marriage, came closest to acknowledging the possibility of such a connection. He proposed that a marital couple might engage in "embraces, kisses, and other touching" for the purpose of showing and fostering mutual love, even though there was a foreseen "risk of pollution" (ejaculation). The very phrasing of Sanchez' thesis makes clear that he was not so temerous as to apply his analysis to *genital* touching (Noonan, 1966:325).

As the influence of Augustinian doctrine lessened, the criterion of a licit sexual act came to be the Thomist criterion of naturalness. It will be recalled that Thomas had regarded a sexual act as natural so long as it involves depositing semen in the vagina. Some theologians expanded this doctrine to condemn as unnatural any attempt to frustrate the procreative end of intercourse, even though semen be properly deposited (Noonan, 1966:366). On this analysis, abortion is again illicit for the same reason that the use of contraceptive methods in intercourse is illicit. Both impede the procreative aspect of intercourse.

It is essentially this doctrine which is held today by the Roman Catholic Church, even though recent developments have deprived it of its ancient rationale and introduced a fatal inconsistency.

One important development is the recognition of a relationship between love and sexual pleasure. Beginning in the latter part of the 19th century, Catholic theologians recognized the expression and fostering of marital love as a legitimate purpose of intercourse (Noonan, 1966:491-504). Since the expression of love in sexual activity is related to the mutual ability to produce expressive modulations of physical sensations which are deeply gratifying, this development in doctrine implies that it is not intrinsically evil to seek sexual pleasure.

I have suggested here that is was a hostility towards sexual pleasure which led to the Church's initial insistence that sex be linked to procreation. Procreation was the value selected to control and, so to speak, to legitimate the experience of sensuous delight in sexual experience. Consequently, if the seeking of sexual pleasure is no longer regarded as sinful, then the initial rationale for maintaining a link between sex and procreation is eliminated.

Although thus deprived of its initial rationale, the traditional Catholic sexual ethic has not been abandoned. Instead, the Catholic Church has continued to modify its description of the precise nature of the link between sex and procreation. This process of modification may be observed in three 20th century papal addresses concerning sex-related issues.

9. In "Casti Connubi" (1930), an encyclical on marriage, Pope Pius XI acknowledged that the cultivation of mutual love is one of the lawful ends of the conjugal act. He immediately subordinated this end to the "primary" end of procreation, however, and harshly condemned any frustration of the latter.

The Divine Majesty, Pius XI (1930:132) said, "regards with greatest detestation this horrible crime and at times has punished it with death." As frustrations of procreation, both contraception and abortion would thus be abominated.

In a subsequent section abortion is denounced, not however as sexual sin, but as violation of the commandment "Thou shalt not kill." Augustine is cited as authority. Of interest is the fact that the citation is a portion of the passage quoted earlier in this chapter (see page 6). It will be recalled that in this passage Augustine rebukes those who abort and those who use contraceptive potions, *not as murderers of innocent human beings, but as sexual sinners.*

10. In 1951 the successor to Pius XI approved a method designed to permit a couple to enjoy sexual relations while avoiding conception, at the same time that he claimed to transmit the traditional rule of conjugal sexual relations. The contraceptive method approved by Pius XII in "The Apostolate of the Midwife" was the rhythm method, developed in the 1920s. [10]

While in "Casti Connubi" Pius XI had approved intercourse during the sterile period, Pius XII approved the *confining* of intercourse to the sterile period, either for a limited time or for the duration of the marriage. However, morally sufficient reasons were required of couples who would make such a decision to remain childless while "satisfying their sensuality." Moreover, no other method of contraception was given approval, and those who were for physical reasons unable to use the rhythm method were advised that their only recourse was complete sexual abstinence. Nevertheless, "The Apostolate of the Midwife" represented a revolutionary departure from traditional Roman Catholic doctrine.

11. In the most recent papal encyclical on marriage, "Humanae Vitae" (1968), equal status was given to the unitive and procreative aspects of sex. It was maintained, however, that there exists an inseparable connection between these two aspects, willed by God and not to be broken by man acting on his own initiative. This encyclical was the response of Paul VI to those pressing for papal approval of contraceptives such as the anti-ovulant pill. [11]

While I do not wish to argue the point here, I believe that approval of rhythm cannot be consistently maintained together with disapproval of other methods of contraception. Married couples who, relying on calendars and thermometers, plan sexual intercourse so that they remain childless throughout their marital life, have assuredly undertaken and accomplished a total separation of the unitive and procreative aspects of their sexual life. [12]

What is important for our purposes, however, is not the consistency of the latest Roman Catholic teaching on sex, but the implication of that teaching for abortion. With reference to the inseparable connection between the unitive and procreative aspects of sex, Paul VI declared that artificial contraception, sterilization, and abortion are all equally excluded as licit means of regulating birth. [13]

12. To summarize this brief history: Augustine held that the only fully lawful sexual act was intercourse performed solely with procreative intent. On

this teaching, having an abortion would ordinarily indicate the existence of a prior sexual sin. The Augustinian view was replaced by the doctrine that it was permissible to engage in intercourse without procreative intent, but wrong to frustrate its procreative power. According to the latest formulation, it is unlawful to separate the unitive and procreative aspects of sexuality. Abortion, of course, constitutes precisely such a separation. Thus throughout the 2000-year history of the Roman Catholic Church, abortion has been linked to sins of a sexual nature. In fact, abortion, along with the much less frequently practiced infanticide, is the only instance in Catholic moral theology in which one who commits the crime of murder simultaneously violates the natural order with respect to sexuality.

In *The Second Sex*, Simone de Beauvoir (1953:458) complains that the Catholic Church has reserved its uncompromising humanitarianism for man in the fetal condition. Should this be true, the explanation may be that in fetal killing two varieties of sin combine.

This presentation of the Roman Catholic condemnation of abortion as a sexual sin need not be carried further, for two reasons. In the first place, it should be evident from the preceding discussion that I find the Catholic ethic of sex unacceptable, in so far as it demands that sexual activity be linked to procreation. If this were the only basis upon which a condemnation of abortion could be defended, I would not find the moral acceptability of abortion in the least problematic. In my view, not only is the Catholic sexual ethic internally inconsistent, without a plausible rationale, and injurious to human love, but it actually conflicts with the other value found in the Catholic condemnation of abortion, namely, protection of fetal life.

A moral theology which recognizes the positive contribution of erotic love to human existence, while seeking to protect fetal life, might *discourage* potentially procreative sex except where accompanied by an intent or at least a willingness to procreate, while *encouraging* sexual activity incapable of procreating. The Catholic Church has proclaimed almost the exact opposite, and has thus created an unconscionable tension between erotic love and the protection of fetal life.

Secondly, even if this singularly Catholic view of sex were defensible, it could not be legitimately promoted as a basis for restrictive abortion legislation. In our religiously and morally pluralistic society, it is generally held that restriction of individual liberty by law is justified only where necessary to protect the rights of other persons, or to ensure the maintenance and stability of society. Enforcement of the Catholic requirement that sex be procreatively-linked could not be justified in either regard. It is implausible to consider the mutually agreeable use of contraceptives in marital intercourse, for example, as endangering either the rights of the spouses, or social stability.[14]

Some Catholics might disagree with this statement of the limited function of law, holding rather that civil law should prohibit where practical whatever is contrary to the divine law as interpreted by the Roman Catholic Church.[15] If this position be taken, however, Catholics are not entitled to deny—as they do—that their support of a constitutional amendment protecting fetal life is an attempt to impose their morality on others.[16] Other religious denominations dispute the claim of the Roman Catholic Church to be the authoritative interpreter of divine law regarding sexual activity.

The reason for including this discussion of abortion as a sin of sex should now be clear. It is essential, in the public debate over a Human Life Amendment, that Roman Catholic spokespersons distinguish scrupulously between abortion as a sin of sex, and abortion as a sin of killing. Abortion as a frustration of procreation is not a legitimate subject of legislative concern; abortion as the killing of a human being assuredly is.

Hence it is misleading, in the context of the present public debate, to maintain that the Roman Catholic Church has *always* condemned abortion.[17] For the greater part of the Church's history, many theologians in fact denied that the fetus is a human being from conception onwards. (See section 15). Thus early abortions were not considered murder, although the medieval tendency to castigate all varieties of sexual sinners as murderers may obscure this point. What is constant in the history of the Roman Catholic Church is rather the excoriation of abortion as sexual sin.

This issue of classification is not a trivial one. That the Church has always condemned abortion as a sin of sex adds no weight whatsoever to Roman Catholic advocacy of a Human Life Amendment. The argument for legal protection of the fetus must be made to stand or fall entirely with the claim that abortion constitutes the wrongful killing of a human being.

13. Consequently, we must move on to an examination of the moral arguments whose source is the Roman Catholic ethic of killing. Before concluding this section, however, I would call attention to yet another sense in which abortion is a sex-related sin.

Catholic teaching maintains that a woman is ordained by nature to find her primary fulfillment in motherhood.[18] It is well known that many of those in the forefront of the push for repeal of abortion laws rejected this view, and saw repeal as necessary to enable a woman to seek primary fulfillment outside the home, or to work out whatever combination of parental and vocational fulfillment she sees fit. Thus the Catholic Church correctly perceives in the abortion movement a threat to its notion of a natural sexual dichotomy. It is not surprising, then, to find the divine origin of sex roles affirmed amid Catholic teaching on abortion.

In "Casti Connubi," for example, Pius XI (1930:138-39) warns that women who focus attention chiefly on their own affairs rather than the home will achieve, to their own detriment, a "false liberty and unnatural equality." The point is put more subtly by Paul VI (1972:335) as he proclaims in "The Right to be Born" that "woman's authentic liberation does not consist in a formalistic or materialistic equality with the other sex, but in recognizing what the female personality has that is essentially specific to it: woman's vocation to be a mother."

Since I find the notion of a natural sexual dichotomy as unacceptable as the Church's sexual ethic, it will not be considered further here as a basis for the immorality of abortion. It too is an unacceptable basis for a Human Life Amendment. In this era of equal rights legislation, it cannot plausibly be argued that a constitutional amendment should be passed for the purpose of reinforcing sex-role stereotypes.

II. Abortion as a Sin of Killing

14. In contrast to the arguments rooted in the Roman Catholic view of sex and sex roles, the Catholic argument against abortion as a sin of killing deserves to be treated with seriousness and respect. That argument is as follows: (1) Abortion involves the killing of a human fetus; (2) A human fetus is, from conception[19] onwards, an innocent human being; (3) It is morally wrong to kill an innocent human being; (4) Consequently, abortion is immoral.[20]

Sometimes the argument is put in terms of a fetal "right to life." Claiming that one of the unalienable rights of every human being is a right to life, and that the fetus is a human being, Roman Catholic doctrine insists upon the right to life of the fetus. It is further claimed that no one can have a contrary right where an innocent human being is concerned, and hence that abortion is morally wrong.[21]

15. No justification is offered in the papal statements for the premise that the fetus is, from conception onwards, a human being. Elsewhere, Roman Catholic writers frequently claim that science demonstrates the humanity of the fetus.

This claim is made, for example, by Robert M. Byrn, a law professor and authority on abortion law.[22] That abortion kills a live human being is, according to Byrn (1973b:513), a secular factual issue which is "resolved beyond cavil by undisputed genetic, biological, fetological evidence."

This is also the position taken by the United States Catholic Conference in public testimony on behalf of a constitutional amendment which would protect fetal life from conception onwards (*Documentation on the Right to Life and Abortion*, 1974:4-9, 37). Similarly, in his introduction of a Human Life Amendment, Senator James Buckley (1974:40) remarks, "It is a question of biological fact as to what constitutes 'human being' and as to when 'offspring' may be said to come into existence."[23] Moreover, it is maintained in "Declaration on Abortion" (1974:256-257), issued by the Sacred Congregation for the Doctrine of the Faith and confirmed by Pope Paul VI, that "Science has shown that from the very first moment [fertilization] this living being possesses a stable structure or genetic program; it is a human being, an individual human being with all its characteristic traits already fixed."

It should be noted that it has not always been the position of the Roman Catholic Church that the fetus is a human being from conception onwards.

The issue was traditionally discussed in terms of the moment at which the fetus is animated or infused with a human soul, and for the greater part of the Church's history the more common opinion was that ensoulment did *not* take place at conception. Hence many theologians believed that an early abortion did not constitute the killing of a human being.

For example, a distinction between an ensouled and an unensouled fetus is implicit in the passage quoted earlier from Augustine (p. 6), although the distinction does not detract from Augustine's condemnation of early abortion and contraception as sexual sin. Augustine affirmed that he did not know when the fetus was ensouled. (Noonan, 1970:15).

Many theologians in the medieval period, Thomas Aquinas included, repeated this distinction. Some invoked it to permit early abortions for reasons which would not justify the killing of a human being. (Noonan, 1970:26-29; Dedek, 1972:38-40).

The distinction was also affirmed in many of the collections of canon law compiled during the medieval period (Huser, 1942:37-57). Based on the stage of fetal development, different penalties for abortion were proposed, e.g., a penance of one year if less than 40 days, three years if over 40 days, and ten years (the punishment for murder) if animation had taken place (Huser, 1942:38). As for the time of animation, it was frequently proposed that the male fetus was animated at 40 days and the (less progressive) female fetus at 80 days (Huser, 1942:55-56).

The *Decretals* of Pope Gregory IX (1227-1241), the first authentic collection of laws for the entire Church, contains a canon specifying that abortion at any point be held as murder. This canon, however, is a version of the passage quoted earlier (p. 7) from the *Decretum* of Buchard, in which not only abortion but also contraception is condemned as homicide (Huser, 1942:50-51; Noonan, 1966:168-169, 178).

In 1588 the papal constitution *Effrenatam* of Sixtus V dismissed the distinction between an ensouled and an unensouled fetus, establishing the penalty of excommunication for both. However, it cannot be inferred from this that Sixtus V regarded early abortion as the killing of a human being, for he also proposed excommunication as a penalty for contraception. In a paraphrase of the passage quoted earlier from Augustine (p. 6), he denounced contraception, together with all abortion, as "cruel lust" (Noonan, 1966:362). Three years later, the successor to Sixtus V repealed the penalty of excommunication for contraception and abortion of an unanimated fetus, retaining the penalty only for abortion of an animated fetus (Huser, 1942:62-63).

In 1869, the distinction between an ensouled and an unensouled fetus was dropped as far as excommunication was concerned. It was not until 1918, however, that all reference to this distinction was eliminated from canon law (Huser, 1942:68-69). By that time, the theory of immediate animation had superseded the theory of delayed animation.

16. It is a recent development in Roman Catholic doctrine, then, to consider the fetus a human being from conception onwards. Once that

position is adopted, however, the Roman Catholic argument against abortion is eminently plausible. If the fetus is a human being, then any justification for taking fetal life must also be a sufficient reason for the killing of those to whom human status is uncontroversially accorded.

Roman Catholic moral theologians point out that it is universally granted that one may not kill one's thirteen-year-old because s/he was conceived as a result of rape, or because s/he lost an arm or leg in an automobile accident, or because care of her/him places a drain on the family's financial resources, interferes with one's pursuits, or endangers one's emotional stability. Similarly, they maintain that it is obvious that such considerations cannot be used to justify abortion.

Moreover, no one who argues that the constitutional right to privacy includes the right of a woman to determine family size has suggested that a woman be permitted, under this right, to kill her school age children. Nor does anyone suggest that a supposed right of the state to control or engineer population growth extends to a right to kill adults or post-natal children should population exceed tolerable limits. It follows, on the Catholic argument, that neither could such supposed rights justify the violation of fetal life.

The Roman Catholic condemnation of abortion as a sin of killing is thus presented as a conclusion validly derived from a moral principle common to our Judaeo-Christian society and a factual premise well established by the scientific developments of the past century. The moral principle is, moreover, one which it is generally agreed should be enforced by law. By advocating restrictive abortion legislation on this basis, Roman Catholics preclude the criticism that they seek to regulate what should rather be left to individual conscience. (By restrictive legislation, I mean state laws or a constitutional amendment which either prohibits abortion entirely, or else would permit it only when necessary to save the life of the pregnant woman.)

17. It is obvious that the questions whether or not the fetus is a human being, and how its status is properly determined, are crucial to assessing the Roman Catholic position. Recently, however, there have been a number of philosophical attempts to assess the Catholic moral/legal position independently of the status of the fetus issue (Bennett, 1971; Brody, 1971, 1973; Foot, 1971; Thomson, 1971). The authors cited assume the humanity of the fetus in order to examine in greater depth the steps according to which the condemnation of abortion is supposed to follow from the imputation of humanity to the fetus. The obvious advantage of such a strategy is that it bypasses the present impasse between those who insist upon the humanity of the fetus and those who deny it.

This strategy is employed in the present study. While assuming for the sake of argument that the fetus is a human being, I will assess the Roman Catholic moral position with regard to three types of abortion. The types of abortion to be considered are as follows: (1) therapeutic abortion (chapters II, III, V), (2) abortion of a fetus resulting from rape (chapter IV), and (3) abortion of a malformed fetus (chapter VI).

Exception to the immorality of abortion has most frequently been urged with regard to these three categories. Legislation incorporating these exceptions was passed by a number of states prior to the Supreme Court decision of 1973. Such so-called "moderate laws" were denounced by most Roman Catholic moralists, who claim that only restrictive abortion legislation is compatible with the universal value of reverence for life. The present study is an attempt to show that this claim is mistaken.

NOTES

[1] This definition is found in the companion abortion case, *Doe v. Bolton,* 410 US 179 (1973).

[2] The Roman Curia is the complex of bureaus through which the Pope implements his judicial, legislative, and executive office as head of the Roman Catholic Church.

[3] The Second Vatican Council (1962-65) was a policy-making assembly of Roman Catholic leadership from all over the world.

[4] In what follows, I rely heavily on Noonan's (1966) monumental study of the history of the Roman Catholic treatment of contraception. Noonan obviously is not responsible for my speculative interpretation of that history.

[5] *Meditations* contains numerous admiring references to Socrates' conduct.

[6] One particularly dramatic passage in the *Phaedo* (83d) compares bodily pleasures to rivets which nail the soul to the body, thereby rendering the soul unfit for the contemplation of truth. This language is easily adaptable to Christian use by a substitution of God for truth.

[7] An exception to the requirement of procreative intent was made in circumstances where intercourse was requested, for whatever reasons, by one's spouse. In such circumstances, a response was permitted and moreover required. This exception in doctrine appears to be aimed at keeping within marital bounds the sexual activity of a spouse who was too "weak" to obey the strict procreative rule. The exception is curious in that it makes it a duty to respond to what it is a sin to initiate. (See *The Good of Marriage*, chs. 6 and 7.)

[8] There is, of course, the possibility that a woman who aborts engaged in intercourse with a procreative intent, but has since changed her mind. Augustine does not consider this possibility.

[9] Noonan (1966:88-90) concludes from a survey of the biological theories of that time that no one believed that the male seed was ensouled, or was itself a human being.

[10] In contrast to the ineffective rhythm method whose use Augustine had condemned, this is a scientifically based and effective method for determining periods of infertility.

[11] See, e.g., "Majority Papal Commission Report," in Callahan (1969).

[12] Evidence may be found in "Humanae Vitae" for the view that the rhythm method commends itself to the Pope because it is the only contraceptive method which requires that spouses periodically stifle their desires for each other.

[13]The reexamination currently underway in some quarters concerning the morality of homosexual relations, premarital sex, and masturbation provoked an urgent declaration by the Vatican, approved by Pope Paul VI, that the Church "transmits without error" the "absolute and immutable" principle concerning the immorality of nonprocreative sex ("Declaration on Certain Questions Concerning Sexual Ethics," 1976). While not mentioning abortion, this document attests to the vitality of the Roman Catholic sexual ethic with regard to which abortion is sexual sin.

[14]In this connection it is relevant to note than in the constitutional challenge presented to Connecticut's law against the use of contraceptive articles, the state did not attempt to argue that the law was justifiable because of the immorality of artificial contraception per se. The state rather presented the argument, rejected by the Court, that the statute bore a rational relation to the much more broadly based value of regulating extramarital sexuality (*Griswold v. Conn.*, 381 US 479, 1965).

[15]For a discussion of the various positions held by Catholics on the relationship between natural law and civil law, see Curran (1973) and Micallef (1972).

[16]For example, in a statement by the National Conference of Catholic Bishops before the Senate subcommittee on constitutional amendments it is claimed that

> ". . . we are not seeking to impose the Catholic moral teaching regarding abortion on the country. . . .
> Furthermore, in a religiously pluralistic society, government is not expected to formulate laws solely on the basis of the religious teaching of any particular Church. In the formulation of law, though, it is appropriate that the convictions of citizens, and the principles from which they are derived, be taken into consideration. There are certain principles of morality taught by the various Churches that are part and parcel of the legal tradition of American society." (*Documentation on the Right to Life and Abortion*, 1974:2-3)

[17]See, e.g., *Documentation on the Right to Life and Abortion* (1974:57, 61) and "Declaration on Abortion" (1974:253).

[18]See, e.g., the article entitled "Women" in the *New Catholic Encyclopedia* (1967). For a detailed historical study and criticism of the Catholic view of women, see Daly (1968).

[19]By "conception" is meant fertilization, the union of sperm and ova.

[20]Two papal documents contain this argument: "Casti Connubi" (Pius XI, 1930:135) and "The Apostolate of the Midwife" (Pius XII, 1951a:163). See also "Declaration on Abortion" (1974:252-255).

[21]The most detailed papal statement of this version of the argument is found in "The Right to be Born" (Paul VI, 1972:333-335). See also Pius XII (1951a:163) and "Declaration on Abortion" (1974:255-257).

[22]Byrn was court-appointed guardian for a class of fetuses in a court action challenging the constitutionality of New York's abortion-on-request law. See *Byrn v. New York City Health and Hosps. Corp.*, 38 App. Div. 2d 306 (1972).

[23]Buckley's amendment provides that "with respect to the right to life, the word 'person,' as used . . . in the Fifth and Fourteenth Articles of Amendment to the Constitution of the United States, applies to all human beings, including their unborn offspring at every stage of their biological development. . . ." That the phrase "from the moment of conception" does not appear in the Buckley amendment, as it does in the Human Life Amendment introduced by Rep. Lawrence Hogan, aroused speculation that Buckley meant to exclude from protection the pre-implantation zygote. In questioning before the subcommittee on constitutional amendments, however, Buckley (1974:88) clearly states his view that medical evidence establishes that fertilization, not implantation, marks the beginning of a human being.

CHAPTER II

The Roman Catholic Doctrine of Therapeutic Abortion

18. Life-threatening pregnancies present a conflict between the life of the pregnant woman and the life of the fetus. What is the moral thing to do in situations of mortal conflict between two innocent human beings? Roman Catholic moral theology has evolved a detailed response to this question in the context of abortion.

It should be acknowledged that with advances in medical technology, such situations infrequently arise in the United States. Ectopic pregnancy, where the embryo implants and develops outside its normal uterine site, is the exception to this statement. Such pregnancies occur frequently—according to one study (Willson *et al.,* 1975:202), at the rate of 1 to every 78 uterine pregnancies. With regard to uterine pregnancies, however, even medical proponents of abortion law liberalization acknowledge that there are few diseases or complications of pregnancy which call for termination of pregnancy in order to save the woman's life. Nevertheless, considerable criticism has been levelled against the traditional Roman Catholic view of what should be done were such situations to arise.

On the basis of the following authoritative statements, one might assume that Catholic doctrine opposes therapeutic abortion. The first statement is from "Casti Connubi," an address by Pope Pius XI (1930:134-5), and the second is from the more recent "Declaration on Abortion" (1974:257) issued by the Sacred Congregation for the Doctrine of the Faith and confirmed by Pope Paul VI.

As to the *medical and therapeutic "indication"* to which, using their own words, We may have made reference, Venerable Brethren, however much We may pity the mother whose health and even *life* is gravely imperiled in the performance of the duty allotted to her by nature, nevertheless what could ever be a sufficient reason for excusing in any way the direct murder of the innocent? This is precisely what we are dealing with here. Whether inflicted upon the mother or upon the child, it is against the precept of God and the law of nature: "Thou shalt not kill." The life of each is equally sacred, and no one has the power, not even the public authority, to destroy it. It is of no use to appeal to the right of taking away life, for here it is a question of the innocent, whereas that right has regard only to the guilty; nor is there here question of defense by bloodshed against an unjust aggressor (for who would call an innocent child an unjust aggressor?); again there is no question here of what is called the "law of extreme necessity" which could never extend to the direct killing of the innocent. *Upright and skillful doctors strive most praiseworthily to guard and preserve the lives of both mother and child; on the contrary, those show themselves most unworthy of the noble medical profession who encompass the death of one or the other, through a pretense at practicing medicine or through motives of misguided pity.* (Italics added)

We must face up to these very serious difficulties: for example, the mother's health, or *even her life*, may be endangered [by pregnancy] . . . .
  Nonetheless we must assert without qualification that *none* of these reasons justifies disposing of the life of another human being, even in its earliest stages. (Italics added)

This assumption, however, is mistaken. While Catholic doctrine does not permit all therapeutic abortions, it does permit *some.* This intriguing distinction among abortions all of which are aimed at preserving the life of the pregnant woman, is the subject of the present chapter. Four obstetrics cases are presented for the purpose of assessing the consistency of the Catholic doctrine of therapeutic abortion. Two of the cases involve situations in which Catholic doctrine permits therapeutic abortion; the other two involve situations in which therapeutic abortion is forbidden. The problem is to determine the difference between the licit and illicit abortions, and whether or not that difference is morally relevant.

Clarification of terminology employed here is in order at this point. The term "fetus" is used to refer to the *conceptus* from fertilization through all subsequent stages of pregnancy. Although the standard medical definition of abortion is the interruption of pregnancy before the fetus is viable (Greenhill and Friedman, 1974:185), it is useful in this study to extend usage of the term to include both the removal of a non-viable fetus and destructive operations in which the death of a viable fetus is a foreseen result.

The term "therapeutic abortion" is used here to refer only to those abortions believed necessary to prevent the "natural" (non-suicidal) death of the woman during pregnancy or shortly thereafter. This is admittedly a departure from common usage, as abortions performed to preserve health and even psychological well-being are frequently called therapeutic. Adoption of this restricted usage is simply for convenience. Since the task is to determine how it is possible to discriminate morally among abortions all of which are undertaken to preserve the woman's life, it is useful to have a term which refers strictly to life-saving abortions.

I. Four Cases of Conflict
between Maternal and Fetal Life[1]

19. Case A. A woman in early pregnancy has invasive cancer of the cervix. If removal of her uterus (hysterectomy) is promptly performed, she has a good chance of survival. The operation will, of course, result in the death of the fetus, whose development would otherwise be normal.[2]

Case B. A woman has a pre-viable pregnancy which is developing in one of her fallopian tubes instead of in her uterus. If an operation is not performed to excise the fetus or remove the tube containing the fetus, she may die from a spontaneous tubal abortion or rupture. Although this operation will result in the death of the fetus, it is extremely unlikely that the fetus could survive in any event.[3]

Case C. A woman in early pregnancy is suffering from chronic hypertensive heart disease associated with severe renal insufficiency. If her pregnancy is not terminated, she may die as a result of the increased demands the pregnancy places on her cardiovascular and renal functions. Although termination of the pregnancy will result in the death of the fetus, its chances for survival are slight in any event.[4]

Case D. A woman in prolonged obstructed labor will die unless an operation is performed in which the head of her unborn fetus is crushed (craniotomy). If craniotomy is not performed and the woman dies from uterine rupture or exhaustion, the fetus will in all likelihood die also.[5]

20. According to standard Catholic doctrine, the physician in case A is permitted to remove the cancerous uterus, even though s/he foresees the death of the non-viable fetus as a certain result. Similarly, in the event of a tubal pregnancy, case B, the fallopian tube may be removed, even though the death of the non-viable fetus is foreseen as an inevitable result. In cases C and D, however, the physician may not operate. S/he may not abort the woman with chronic hypertension, and may not perform a craniotomy on a living fetus.[6]

21. Catholic moralists do not justify their judgments on the basis of the probabilities of maternal/fetal survival. It should be observed that it would not be possible to do so. Consider fetal survival, for instance. It might be supposed that abortion of a tubal pregnancy, case B, is permissible because of the extremely slight chance that the fetus could be delivered alive in any event. However, the same may be said of case C, where therapeutic abortion is not permissible.

Nor can it be supposed that maternal mortality is the critical factor. Many women survive tubal pregnancy without the surgical intervention which is licit according to Catholic moral theology.[7] On the other hand, a woman will certainly die if her obstructed labor is not relieved, yet craniotomy—in past times the only way of relieving certain abnormalities of labor—is forbidden by Catholic doctrine.[8] In order to justify the moral discriminations made among these cases, it is evident that appeal must be made to factors other than the chances of maternal/fetal survival.

To account for the moral discriminations among these cases, Catholic moralists invoke the important principle of Catholic moral theology called the Principle of Double Effect. We turn now to an examination of that principle.

II. The Principle of Double Effect

22. The Principle of Double Effect is used by Catholic moralists to identify those situations in which it is morally permissible to aim at a good effect, even though evil is also a foreseen consequence of one's actions. The principle is aptly termed "Double Effect," as two effects, one good and one bad, are involved. This principle is applied frequently in contemporary Catholic treatment of such topics as abortion, sterilization, prolongation of life, suicide and conduct in war.[9]

The following statement of the Principle of Double Effect by Farraher (1963:71), given equivalent formulations by Callahan (1970:423) and Granfield (1971:127-8) is typical:

An act having the double effect of a good and an evil consequence is permissible where

    (1) the immediate action performed be good or indifferent;
    (2) the foreseen evil effect be not intended in itself;
    (3) the good which is intended be not an effect of the evil;
    (4) the good intended be commensurate with the evil foreseen.

Catholic moralists maintain that abortion in cases A and B satisfies the Principle of Double Effect, and hence is licit. By contrast, abortion in cases C and D is said to violate the conditions of that principle, and hence to be illicit.[10]

23. In a therapeutic abortion, the foreseen *evil* effect is of course the death of the fetus, and the *good* effect is the preservation of the pregnant woman's life. Condition (4) of the Principle of Double Effect requires that the good and bad effects be commensurate or proportional. Since the good effect and the bad effect are the same for every therapeutic abortion, it is evident that condition (4) cannot be used to make moral discriminations among therapeutic abortions. Catholic moralists regard preservation of the woman's life as commensurate with fetal death, and hence regard condition (4) as satisfied by all therapeutic abortions. (An example of an operation which would clearly violate this condition is the removal of a small ovarian cyst in a pregnant woman. Catholic moralists would not consider the slight benefit to the woman's health to be commensurate with the risk of loss of fetal life.)

24. Associated with the Principle of Double Effect is a distinction between evil effects brought about *directly* and those brought about *indirectly*. The Principle of Double Effect is said to forbid direct killing, for example, but to permit some instances of indirect killing. With regard to therapeutic abortion, licit therapeutic abortions are said to involve indirect killing of the fetus, whereas in the illicit ones the fetus is said to be killed directly. Pius XI alludes to this distinction in the passage quoted earlier (section 18) from "Casti

Connubi," which had at first sight appeared to condemn all therapeutic abortions.

> As to the medical and therapeutic "indication" to which, using their own words, We have made reference, Venerable Brethren, however much We may pity the mother whose health and even life is gravely imperiled in the performance of the duty allotted to her by nature, nevertheless what could ever be a sufficient reason for excusing in any way the *direct* murder of the innocent? (Italics added)

Similarly, it is stated in the recent "Declaration on Abortion" (1974:257) that nothing could ever justify the *direct* killing of the innocent. These remarks, while leaving open the possibility that indirect killing could be excused, emphasize that direct killing is always forbidden even for the commensurately serious reason of saving the life of the pregnant woman. We may infer that the characterization of fetal killing as direct or indirect is independent of condition (4), and depends upon conditions (1), (2), or (3), or some combination of these.

25. But condition (2) of the Principle of Double Effect cannot be used to distinguish among therapeutic abortions, for in no case is the foreseen evil effect, fetal death, intended in itself. It is manifest that the end for which therapeutic abortion is undertaken is not fetal death but preservation of the life of the pregnant woman. That leaves conditions (1) and (3) as possible bases for the moral discriminations among therapeutic abortions.

26. Papal pronouncements may be cited to suggest that it is condition (3) which serves to distinguish licit from illicit therapeutic abortions. Pius XII, for example, in "The Apostolate of the Midwife" (1951a:163), defines a *direct* attack upon human life as an action which "aims at its [life's] destruction either as an end in itself or as the means of attaining another end that is perhaps in no way illicit in itself."[11] This passage suggests that killing is *indirect* where death is neither an end nor a means to an end. Thus, according to Pius XII, an indirect killing satisfies conditions (2) and (3) of the Principle of Double Effect, whereas a direct killing violates one or the other of these conditions. It will be recalled that all therapeutic abortions satisfy condition (2). (See section 25.) It follows that on the formulation of direct and indirect killing provided by Pius XII, licit therapeutic abortions are distinguishable from illicit ones with reference to condition (3) of the Principle of Double Effect.

27. This third condition is certainly the key to understanding many applications of the Principle of Double Effect. Consider, for example, Catholic doctrine on the morality of procedures which induce sterility. Catholic moralists use the Principle of Double Effect to explain why they condemn an oophorectomy (removal of the ovaries) performed to prevent conception, while they approve of the same procedure when performed to rid the patient of numerous ovarian cysts. In the first case, they consider the sterilization direct; in the second, indirect. (See, e.g., Kelly, 1958:183-9; *Ethical and Religious Directives for Catholic Health Facilities*, 1971: sections 18, 20).

The foreseen bad effect in both cases is, of course, the patient's sterility. Moreover, in both cases preservation of physical health may be the desired good effect. That is, an oophorectomy might be performed on non-cystic ovaries because it was believed that a future pregnancy would endanger the woman's life or health.

The cases may be distinguished, however, in the following way. In the first case, where oophorectomy is illicit, sterility *is a means* to the desired end of preserving the patient's health. Sterility is the means chosen for the prevention of physically hazardous pregnancies. In the instance of licit oophorectomy, on the other hand, sterility is *not a means* of preserving the patient's health, but only a *foreseen* by-product of the means chosen to that end. If this distinction isn't clear, try imagining the examples with a few more details. Suppose that (a) in both cases the surgeon believes that only one ovary is functioning; (b) in the second case (involving ovarian cysts), it is the functioning ovary which is cystic; and (c) consequently, in both cases the surgeon removes only the functioning ovary. If the remaining ovary begins to function after the operation, it should be evident that only in the first case, where the patient's sterility is a means to the desired end, would the surgeon re-operate.

The use of pills which suppress ovulation is treated similarly in Catholic moral theology. In response to whether or not it is licit to use such remedies for uterine pathologies when they also make conception impossible, Pius XII (1958:395) applies the Principle of Double Effect as follows:

> The answer depends on the intention of the person. If a woman takes such medicine, not to prevent conception, but only on the advice of a doctor as a necessary remedy because of the condition of the uterus or the organism, she produces *indirect* sterilization, which is permitted according to the general principles governing acts with a double effect. But a *direct* and, therefore, illicit sterilization results when ovulation is stopped to protect the uterus and the organism from the consequences of a pregnancy which it is not able to sustain. Some moralists contend that it is permissible to take medicines with this latter intention, but they are in error.
>
> It is likewise necessary to reject the view of a number of doctors and moralists who permit these practices when medical indications make conception undesirable, or in other similar cases, which cannot be discussed here. In these cases the use of medication has as its end the prevention of conception by preventing ovulation. They are instances, therefore, of direct sterilization.

Again, sterilization is illicit where the bad effect is a *means* to the preservation of the woman's health, and licit where the bad effect is not the means but a *foreseen* consequence of the means chosen. (We may thus refer to this distinction as the *means/foresight* distinction.)

Another striking example is the Catholic position on the alleviation of pain by medications which simultaneously hasten death. Medical ethics texts condemn the physician who would seek to arrest the suffering of a terminal cancer patient by administering a fatal air injection, even if the patient has requested it. Yet traditional Catholic doctrine permits a physician to authorize increased dosage of pain-reducing medication even when doing so will predictably result in the patient's death. Again, from Pius XII (1957a:48):

If, between the narcosis and the shortening of life, there exists no direct causal link, imposed either by the intention of the interested parties or by the nature of things (as would be the case if the suppression of the pain could be obtained only by the shortening of life), and if, on the contrary, the administration of narcotics produces two distinct effects, one, the relief of pain and the other, the shortening of life, then the action is lawful; however, it must be determined whether there is a reasonable proportion between these two effects and whether the advantages of the one effect compensate for the disadvantages of the other.

Although in either case the physician may be said to have killed the patient for reasons of mercy, Catholic authorities regard the administration of such pain therapy as distinct from euthanasia.[12] On their view, euthanasia, which is always forbidden, involves an attempt to end suffering with *death as a means*. Again, the Principle of Double Effect is used to forbid those acts in which the bad effect is a means to the good effect, and permit those in which it is not.

A final example comes from Häring. After expressing the standard Catholic doctrine that suicide is immoral, Häring writes that although the Japanese kamikaze pilots could not but lose their lives, they did not commit suicide because "Their direct intention . . . was not self-destruction but a noble military gesture that demanded self-sacrifice." (1973:72).

28. Condition (3), or the means/foresight distinction, is thus the key to understanding many applications of the Double Effect Principle. Reflection upon the four obstetrics cases will show, however, that condition (3) cannot be the key to understanding the application of the Double Effect Principle to therapeutic abortion.

Consider an instance in which therapeutic abortion is licit—case A, for example. This is the case of the pregnant woman with the cancerous cervix. Since removal of her uterus is licit, one would expect that in this instance the operating surgeon does not aim at fetal death either as an end or as a means to the desired end. And indeed this would appear to be true. As stated previously, the end aimed at is manifestly preservation of the woman's life. And the means to this end is not fetal death, but rather removal of the woman's uterus. Death of the non-viable fetus is a by-product of this means. Should the fetus, contrary to expectation, be removed alive, there would be no point in killing it. This may be contrasted with an instance where a person's death is truly aimed at as a means. Imagine a gunman hired to kill a person in order to prevent that person from revealing certain information. Should the victim, contrary to expectation, survive the first attempt upon her/his life, another attempt would be made.

But the same may be said of case C, where therapeutic abortion is illicit. This is the case of the pregnant woman suffering from chronic hypertension. Here it is removal of the fetus, not its death, which is the means to the end of saving the woman's life. Again, there would be no point in killing the fetus should it, contrary to expectation, be removed alive. That the fetus be removed dead rather than alive serves no end of the doctor, or of the woman.

Even in the forbidden case of craniotomy, case D, fetal death is not a means to the desired end. Some Catholic writers have claimed otherwise. For instance, Kenny (1962:192) states in reference to craniotomy that "The person who performs the operation necessarily *wills* the death of the child either as a *means* of saving the mother's life or because he judges it to be the lesser of two evils."

It is not, however, the death of the fetus that is required for the woman's survival, but the narrowing of the fetus' head sufficiently to prevent the hemorrhaging and exhaustion which will bring about her death. That the narrowing of the head and not the death of the fetus is the means to this end is demonstrated by the fact that the fetus would not be killed should it somehow survive the force applied to its skull and be removed alive from the birth canal. Paul Ramsey (1971:21) expresses this point by saying that "the intention of this action is not the killing, not the death of the fetus," but rather the "*incapacitation* of the fetus from doing what it is doing to the life of the mother."

It would appear then that in any abortion undertaken strictly to prevent the "natural" (non-suicidal) death of the woman during pregnancy or shortly thereafter, the death of the fetus is a foreseen consequence of the means chosen, but is not itself a means to an end. If this conclusion is correct, then all therapeutic abortions satisfy condition (3) of the Principle of Double Effect.

29. It may be noted that this point is obscured by the failure of some Catholic authors to distinguish in a consistent way between the removal of the fetus from the woman's body and its subsequent death. For instance, Gerald Kelly (1955:12) writes that therapeutic abortion in the case of a woman with a cancerous cervix is licit, for "it is the removal of the cancer, *not the death of the fetus*, that saves the woman's life." In other words, Kelly disapproves only of those procedures in which the death of the fetus is the means to the desired end. On the other hand, he writes that the removal of a non-viable fetus as a last resort in a case of *hyperemesis gravidarum* (severe vomiting) is not licit, because the vomiting "is stopped only by the *emptying of the uterus*" (Italics added here and in the above quotation). This suggests the alternative interpretation that Kelly disapproves of those procedures in which the *removal of the fetus* occurs as a means to the end.

In fact, neither view is satisfactory. As I have just argued, the view that a therapeutic abortion is immoral only where *fetal death* is a means to an end is incompatible with making moral distinctions among the four obstetrics cases listed in section 19, distinctions which Kelly himself makes. The second view, that therapeutic abortions are immoral only where *removal of the fetus* is a means to an end, also runs into difficulty. This view presupposes that removal of the fetus is evil, otherwise there would be no reason to condemn its employment as a means to a good end. What makes removal of a non-viable fetus evil, however, is precisely that it results in fetal death. Catholic moralists do not disapprove of removal of a viable fetus for therapeutic reasons. To be consistent, then, any surgical procedure which inevitably results in fetal death should be forbidden as a means. But removal of a cancerous pregnant uterus prior to viability of the fetus is as inevitably associated with fetal death as removal of a non-viable fetus by itself. Consequently, adoption of the second view is again incompatible with the distinctions Kelly and traditional Catholic moralists draw among therapeutic abortions.

30. On the basis of the discussion thus far, we may criticize an interpretation of the Principle of Double Effect provided by Leonard Geddes (1973). Geddes claims that the essence of the Principle of Double Effect is to distinguish between the *intended* and the *merely foreseen* consequences of a voluntary action. [13] Death is an *intended* consequence of an action, Geddes says, where the action aims at death either as an end in itself, or as a means to an end. A killing is *intentional* where death is intended. In voluntary but *non-intentional* killing, on the other hand, death is a foreseen (though not intended) consequence.

There is a broader sense of intended which may be more in accord with ordinary usage than this narrow sense provided by Geddes. Hart (1968:120) suggests that in ordinary usage one does intentionally what one sets out to achieve, either as a means or an end, as well as what is "so immediately and invariably connected with the action done that the suggestion that the action might not have had that outcome would by ordinary standards be regarded as absurd."

Let us examine the possibility that the Principle of Double Effect is meant to distinguish between the intended and merely foreseen consequences of a voluntary action, in one or the other of these two senses of intended. If Hart's broad sense of intended be adopted, it follows that any and all cases of therapeutic abortion would count as intentional killing. That is, the connection between the removal of a cancerous uterus containing a non-viable fetus and the death of the fetus is as close as the connection between crushing the head of the unborn child and the resultant death of that child. To suggest that a six-week fetus might have survived removal of the uterus would by ordinary standards be regarded as absurd. Similarly, one could not, in Hart's interpretation, understand Catholic moral discriminations between the pairs of examples considered in section 27.

But a parallel difficulty is encountered if Geddes' narrow sense of intended be adopted. If the preceding discussion is correct, it follows that no cases of therapeutic abortion would count as intentional killing, for in no case is fetal death sought as either means or end. Geddes himself acknowledges this with regard to craniotomy, the single instance of therapeutic abortion considered by him.

Thus, whichever sense of intended be adopted, we have the problem of accounting for the fact that the Principle of Double Effect has traditionally been used to distinguish permissible from forbidden cases of therapeutic abortion.

Of course, one might conclude that Geddes' interpretation of the Principle of Double Effect is correct, and that Catholic moralists have simply erred in applying the Double Effect Principle to therapeutic abortion. This conclusion has some plausibility. In its support are the facts that (1) the intention/foresight distinction, as construed by Geddes, is indeed crucial in other applications of the Double Effect Principle (see section 27); and (2) some Catholic moralists believe that they are using this intention/foresight distinction in their discrimination among therapeutic abortions. We shall not, however, conclude that Catholic moralists have simply misapplied the Principle of Double Effect until we have exhausted all accounts of the basis for distinguishing among therapeutic abortions.

31. In a recent publication on abortion, David Granfield (1971) endorses the standard Catholic doctrine on therapeutic abortion, and yet inconsistently appears to regard a therapeutic abortion as indirect, and hence permissible, where fetal death is not the means whereby the woman is saved. Granfield (1971:132) offers the additional explanation that in the permissible cases of therapeutic abortion, "there is almost invariably, a factor which turns the balance of equality in favor of the mother: namely, that if the operation is not performed, both the mother and the child will die, but if it is performed, the mother will probably live." This won't do, however. As noted earlier (see section 19), fetal survival is highly improbable in case D, where abortion is not permitted. [14] And it is likely that the fetus will survive the woman's cancer of the cervix, a case where abortion *is* permitted.

32. Another moral theologian, Charles E. Curran (1970:238), reports that Catholic moralists have generally agreed that "when the *sole immediate effect* of the action is killing the action is direct killing and therefore wrong" (Italics added). In the case of removal of a cancerous uterus or fallopian tube, Curran says that theologians hold that the action does not tend immediately to the expulsion of the fetus but to the curing of a pathological condition. The same formulation occurs in *Ethical and Religious Directives for Catholic Health Facilities* (1971:section 12), which declares illicit "Every procedure whose sole immediate effect is the termination of pregnancy before viability . . ."[15] By contrast,

> Operations, treatments, and medications, which do not directly intend termination of pregnancy but which have as their purpose the cure of a proportionately serious pathological condition of the mother, are permitted when they cannot be safely postponed until the fetus is viable, even though they may or will result in the death of the fetus. (Section 13)

It should be emphasized that every therapeutic abortion is directed to the achieving of some effect besides fetal death, namely, preservation of the woman's life. In no therapeutic abortion is fetal death the sole effect. Nor can it be supposed that in illicit but not licit therapeutic abortions, fetal death is the sole immediate effect in the sense of being temporally prior to the life-preserving effect. When a forbidden craniotomy is performed, for instance, it would seem that fetal death and prevention of uterine rupture are simultaneous effects. And in the licit case of removal of a cancerous uterus, fetal death may occur simultaneously with or shortly after the life-preserving excision of cancerous tissue. Thus any attempt to make discriminations among therapeutic abortions in terms of the temporal sequence of their good and bad effects seems misguided from the outset, quite apart from the further question of what possible moral relevance such discriminations could have. If, however, by immediate effect is not meant the effect which is first in time but rather the effect which is intended, then we are back to the original problem.

33. In the same year that Pius XII characterizes a killing as indirect in which death is the aim neither as means nor end, he offers in another address a quite different criterion of indirect killing. In "Morality in Marriage" (1951b:189) he says:

> On purpose We have always used the expression "direct attempt on the life of an innocent person," "direct killing." Because if, for example, the saving of the life of the future mother, *independently of her pregnant state*, should urgently require a surgical act or other therapeutic treatment which would have as an accessory consequence, in no way desired or intended but inevitable, the death of the fetus, such act could no longer be called a direct attempt on an innocent life.[16] (Italics added)

This criterion of indirect killing also appears in the writings of Charles Curran. According to Curran (1970:240), some theologians have proposed as a rule of thumb that abortion is indirect "if the action could be done without killing the fetus or if the procedure would be done if the fetus is present or not." The rule of thumb proposed in the first half of the sentence may be set aside as it fails to discriminate between the licit and illicit cases of therapeutic abortion, all of which usually result in fetal death. Contained in the second half of the sentence, however, is another rule of thumb according to which the procedures involved in licit abortions would be done *regardless* of the presence of the fetus. It is plausible to regard such procedures as required independently of pregnancy, thus connecting Curran's second rule of thumb with the papal criterion above.

34. According to that papal criterion, what types of therapeutic abortion count as direct killing? It is plausible to regard craniotomy and abortion in the case of a woman suffering from chronic hypertension as direct killing since each involves a threat to the woman's life clearly related to, rather than independent of, her pregnancy or its circumstances. Removal of the cancerous uterus of a pregnant woman, on the other hand, would count as indirect destruction of innocent life since its removal would be medically indicated whether or not the woman was pregnant. Thus far, application of the criterion provides results consistent with the doctrine on therapeutic abortion found in the manuals of medical ethics.

35. Application of the criterion in the case of ectopic pregnancy, however, proves to be more troublesome. It would seem evident that the threat to a woman's life caused by an ectopic pregnancy is *not* independent of that pregnancy, and consequently that removal of a fallopian tube cannot be justified under this criterion of indirect killing. Nevertheless, in his study of abortion in canon law, Huser (1942:136) says that "almost every ectopic pregnancy will, sooner or later, engender a pathological condition which then, *independently of the pregnancy itself*, constitutes a serious danger to the mother's life" (Italics added).

36. In order to understand this surprising claim it is necessary to refer to an influential study by T. Lincoln Bouscaren (1944) on the morality of ectopic operations. Prior to Bouscaren's study no consensus existed concerning the morality of surgical intervention in a tubal pregnancy before the tube had actually ruptured. Once rupture had occurred, the physician was permitted to treat the acute medical emergency by removing the tube and its contents.

Bouscaren points out that the objection to removal of the tube prior to rupture was based on the mistaken assumption that the tube remained sound until the moment of its actual rupture. Bouscaren introduces medical evidence showing that, on the contrary, the tube begins to deteriorate well before it actually bursts. Placental cells which would normally penetrate the thick mucous lining of the uterus instead penetrate the thin wall of the fallopian tube. This "burrowing in" action of the fetus, even in early pregnancy, results in perforation of blood vessels and dissection of muscles in the tube wall. When rupture occurs, the major cause is not the mechanical inability of the wall to stretch sufficiently to accommodate the growing fetus but the erosion of the tubal wall (Woodruff and Pauerstein, 1969:199).

Thus, Bouscaren is able to claim that from the early stages of pregnancy the tube itself is weakened and dangerous, quite apart from any further development of the pregnancy. On this basis Bouscaren concludes that removal of an unruptured pregnant tube constitutes *indirect* killing since the *direct* object of the operation is removal of a pathological organ of the woman's body. This conclusion was inconsistent with a 1902 decree of the Holy Office[17] which explicitly forbade removal of immature ectopic fetuses. Theologians following Bouscaren maintain, however, that the 1902 decree was correctly based upon the medical facts as then known, but is no longer applicable in the light of subsequent medical research (Grisez, 1970a:180; Kelly, 1958:108-9; Healy, 1956:221-6).

37. We may now return to the criterion of indirect killing proposed by Pius XII (1951b:189) in "Morality in Marriage." It will be recalled that in this address he characterizes fetal killing as indirect if the treatment killing the fetus is required independently of the woman's pregnant condition (Section 33). Now it would clearly be a mistake to conclude from Bouscaren's study that removal of a pregnant fallopian tube is medically indicated independently of pregnancy. Although it is true that at some point prior to rupture the tube becomes dangerous in itself, it is the pregnancy which *causes* the pathological alterations of the tube. Nevertheless, it is possible to see how such a conclusion might be drawn. Bouscaren shows that after a certain point in tubal pregnancy the tube would have to be removed even if the fetus were no longer present. That the tube would have to be removed even if the fetus *were no longer present* might mistakenly be thought to imply that the tube would have to be removed even if the fetus *had not been present*.

To put the point another way, Bouscaren showed that if the fallopian tube of a non-pregnant woman were to undergo pathological changes similar to those occurring in tubal pregnancy, it would have to be removed. Just as any other part of the body, the fallopian tube is subject to infection and tumors, either of which can cause deterioration similar to that occurring in tubal pregnancy.[18] Consequently there are reasons for removing the fallopian tube of a woman who is not pregnant, just as there are reasons for removing the uterus of a woman who is not pregnant. But the fact that a fallopian tube could deteriorate and require excision as a result of factors other than a tubal pregnancy does not mean that the deterioration is independent of the pregnancy when there *is* one. The fundamental reason for removing a pregnant tube is manifestly *that the tube contains a misplaced fetus*. That particular tube would not be removed at that particular time if the fetus were not present. By contrast, the reason for removing a pregnant cancerous uterus is *that the uterus is cancerous, not that it contains a fetus*.

38. When these confusions have been removed, however, one is left with the following facts. Both pregnant and non-pregnant women may have cancer of the cervix, and the fallopian tubes of either may deteriorate. When such pathological conditions arise, the medical remedy is the same for the non-pregnant women as it is for the pregnant women: remove the diseased organ. The situation is quite different with regard to a pregnant woman suffering from chronic hypertension or an obstructed labor. Although a non-pregnant woman may have chronic hypertension, the medical remedy indicated for her cannot be removal of her fetus, for she doesn't have one. And a non-pregnant woman cannot be in obstructed labor at all.

39. One may hazard a guess that these facts are exploited in application of the Principle of Double Effect to therapeutic abortion. According to the formulation in section 22, four conditions establish an act as an instance of permissible killing:

(1) That the immediate action performed be good or indifferent;
(2) That the foreseen evil (fetal death) be not intended in itself;
(3) That the good (preservation of the woman's life) which is intended be not an effect of the evil (fetal death); and
(4) That the good (preservation of the woman's life) be commensurate with the evil (fetal death) foreseen.

It should be clear from previous discussion that conditions (2)-(4) fail to distinguish permissible from non-permissible cases of therapeutic abortion. That leaves condition (1) as a possible basis for distinguishing among therapeutic abortions. It has been argued that it is impossible to distinguish among therapeutic abortions in terms of the temporal priority of their good and bad effects. Adoption of another sense of immediate, however, may provide a solution to the problem.

Observe that removal of a diseased organ from a *non*-pregnant woman cannot result in fetal death. Instead removal is unambiguously life-preserving, and thus has positive moral value. Suppose, now, that one were to describe "the immediate action performed" in removal of a pregnant cancerous uterus or pregnant fallopian tube as *the removal of a diseased organ of the woman's body.* Suppose further that one were to transfer the positive moral value such operations acquire in ordinary contexts to the special context of pregnancy. If this were done, some therapeutic abortions would satisfy condition (1) of the Principle of Double Effect whereas others wouldn't. Specifically, therapeutic abortion in cases A and B would satisfy this condition, while therapeutic abortion in cases C and D would not. "Crushing the head of a fetus," or "removal of a non-viable fetus" are comparable descriptions of immediate actions whose consequences always include the bad effect of loss of life. Consequently, the distinction comes to this: In the case of permissible therapeutic abortion there exists a description of what the surgeon does such that, considered under this description, the surgeon's action in *other* contexts is solely life-preserving. In the case of illicit therapeutic abortion no comparable description is available.

40. Consideration of the following case suggests a more precise formulation of this conclusion. Suppose a woman in early pregnancy suffering from chronic hypertension (case C) also has benign uterine tumors. According to the preceding analysis, removal of her non-viable fetus is illicit. However, the presence of uterine tumors in non-pregnant women is an indication for hysterectomy. Consequently, it might appear licit to terminate her pregnancy by hysterectomy.

In analyzing this case, however, it must be observed that uterine tumors are usually a threat to health but not to life. Consequently, while Catholic moralists would describe fetal killing as indirect if a hysterectomy were performed to rid the woman of uterine tumors, they would probably not consider the gain to health from ridding her body of tumors to be commensurate with loss of fetal life. Certainly this would be true where the benefit to her health was small.

We may now formulate more precisely the difference between licit and illicit therapeutic abortions. Licit abortions meet the following conditions:

(1') fetal death occurs as a result of medical procedures employed to modify *life-threatening* conditions which can occur apart from pregnancy and which, if they did occur apart from pregnancy, would necessitate employment of similar procedures (for brevity of exposition, procedures which satisfy this description will hereafter be referred to as *standard procedures*);

(2) the foreseen evil effect is not intended in itself;

(3) the good which is intended is not an effect of the evil;

(4) the good intended is commensurate with the evil foreseen.

On this interpretation, the only difference between licit and illicit therapeutic abortions is that the licit ones involve *standard procedures* whereas the illicit ones do not. That is, in a licit therapeutic abortion fetal death occurs as a result of a standard medical procedure, as defined above; in illicit therapeutic abortion, it does not. We may refer to the distinction embodied in (1') as the *standard/non-standard procedures* distinction. Our investigation suggests, then, that it is not the means/foresight distinction but the standard/non-standard procedures distinction which accounts for the orthodox Catholic doctrine of therapeutic abortion.

41. That the standard/non-standard procedures distinction has no moral relevance should be evident. Therapeutic abortions satisfying condition (1′) involve medical procedures which are exclusively life-preserving in ordinary contexts but which in the context of pregnancy have both life-preserving and life-destroying consequences. Removal of a cancerous uterus, for instance, has a positive value in ordinary contexts *because* its foreseen consequences are exclusively life-preserving. Thus in appraising its moral value in the context of pregnancy, it cannot be considered *apart from* its foreseen consequences which in this case include fetal death. That is, it is morally irrelevant that removal of a cancerous uterus has purely beneficial effects in *other* contexts when in the context in question it has the same foreseen effects as any procedure of therapeutic abortion. However, on the assumption that Catholic moralists *do* employ the Double Effect Principle to make such spurious distinctions, sense can be made of application of the principle to a number of cases.

42. Consider, for example, the striking illustration of the doctrine presented in Häring's (1970) discussion of abortion. Häring describes an incident recounted to him by a gynecologist who removed a benign uterine tumor from a woman four months pregnant. On the womb the doctor encountered numerous very thin and fragile varicose veins which bled profusely, and whose bleeding was only aggravated by suturing. Two means of preventing the woman's death from loss of blood were available: (1) removal of the bleeding uterus with the fetus inside; (2) removal of the fetus from the uterus, whereupon the bleeding would be stopped by contraction of the uterus. Death of the fetus would result in either case. Thinking that the fetus could not be saved in any event and that preservation of the woman's fertility was desirable, the gynecologist chose the latter course. He was later told by "a noted Catholic moral theologian" (unidentified by Häring) that the course he chose was objectively wrong. According to the gynecologist, "I would have been allowed to remove the bleeding uterus with the fetus itself," he said, "but was not permitted to interrupt the pregnancy while leaving the womb intact. This latter," he said, "constituted an immoral termination of pregnancy, though done for the purpose of saving the mother, while the other would have been a lawful direct intention and action to save life" (1970:136).

It is instructive to note the similarity between the sanctioned removal of the uterus containing the fetus and the forbidden removal of the fetus from the uterus. Both procedures have the negative and undesired effect of fetal death; both have the positive and desired effect of preservation of maternal life. In neither case is the negative effect the means to the positive one. The procedures are similar in their physical aspects except that the first involves the removal of an additional piece of tissue. That variation in physical detail, however, allows description of what the surgeon does in terms of a standard medical procedure which in other contexts lacks the negative effect of fetal death (although it does of course have the negative effect of loss of fertility). That is, in the second case the surgeon removes a non-viable fetus, whereas in the first case he removes a dangerously hemorrhaging uterus.

43. Still another striking application of the Principle of Double Effect confirms this interpretation and illustrates the extraordinary detail of which the Catholic analysis is capable. In an extremely rare type of ectopic pregnancy a fetus which has been growing in the fallopian tube will, after spontaneous abortion or rupture of the tube, pass into the abdominal cavity. The fetus may reimplant on the external surface of the bowel, ovary, uterus, or liver, or in the lining of the body wall, and continue to grow. This condition is known as secondary abdominal pregnancy, and as in tubal pregnancy, the chances of fetal survival are slight (Greenhill and Friedman, 1974:359).

The morality of intervention in such cases is also considered in Bouscaren's study. As mentioned earlier, Bouscaren concludes that it is licit under the Principle of Double Effect to remove an unruptured fallopian tube containing a non-viable fetus. This conclusion rests upon the medical finding that the tube undergoes deterioration prior to rupture. On the other hand, a fetus growing in the abdominal cavity presents a rather different problem. As Bouscaren (1944:164) queries, "Where, in this case, is the dangerous organ which must be the *direct object of the operation?*" In his view, to remove the fetus while leaving intact the tissues or organs to which the fetus is attached would be a direct attack upon the fetus. Yet an abdominal pregnancy is dangerous not so much because of changes in the tissue but because it will probably terminate in a spontaneous abortion involving severe hemorrhage. Hence it is not possible to describe the tissues as themselves diseased. Bouscaren is thus led to conclude that although it would have been permissible to operate while the fetus was growing in the fallopian tube, once the fetus has moved into the abdominal cavity an attempt to remove it cannot be justified.[19]

It seems peculiar that the morality of killing a misplaced fetus depends solely upon the fetus' location in the woman's body, when this factor is not significantly related either to its life-chances or to the threat that it poses to the woman's life. Nevertheless this is to be expected in an approach which fixes on whether or not the fetus is killed by a standard medical procedure.

In qualifying his condemnation of abortion in secondary abdominal pregnancy, Bouscaren only reinforces this point. Bouscaren states that in the crisis of spontaneous detachment of the placenta and consequent hemorrhaging, it is permissible to kill the fetus in the process of *attending to the hemorrhage*. That is, the physician may treat the hemorrhage by ligation of the maternal blood vessels. The by-product of this procedure is the death of the fetus through deprivation of its blood supply. The physician may not, however, remove the fetus from its site in the abdominal cavity prior to such hemorrhage. By thus waiting to act until a hemorrhage occurs, the physician again insures that he kill the fetus only through the use of a standard medical procedure—that is, one which would also be indicated were hemorrhaging to occur in a non-pregnant woman.[20]

44. In this connection, it is interesting to note a discussion by Kelly (1958:84-89) on the general problem of hemorrhaging in inevitable spontaneous abortion. The problem Kelly poses is whether or not ergot preparations may be used when it is foreseen that their use will very likely shear off the placenta and thus hasten the death of the fetus. Kelly concludes that the use of ergot is morally permissible in such cases provided nothing can be done to save the fetus and control the hemorrhaging. The point here is that Kelly's conclusion is based on the fact that as ergot acts to produce uterine contractions, its principal use is to stop uterine hemorrhaging regardless of pregnancy. In prescribing ergot in an inevitable spontaneous abortion, then, the physician is employing the medical treatment indicated by the condition—uterine hemorrhaging—with the death of the fetus simply an unavoidable by-product of the uterine contractions induced by the drug.

Had ergot been found to control hemorrhaging in pregnant women through the expulsion of the fetus rather than through the production of uterine contractions, it is clear that Kelly's conclusion would have had to have been different. That is, should ergot lack hemorrhage-controlling capacity in non-pregnant women, its use to control hemorrhage in pregnant women would not be standard medical procedure, and condition (1') of the Principle of Double Effect would not be satisfied.

Although Kelly does not consider the question explicitly, he implies disapproval of the use of ergot to expel the fetus of a woman whose life was threatened by a non-hemorrhaging pregnancy. Again, the use of ergot in this case would not be standard medical procedure as the term is used here, since ergot would not be used on a non-hemorrhaging, non-pregnant woman.

45. If the interpretation of the Principle of Double Effect offered here is correct, it follows that the fallopian tube *must* be removed along with the fetus in a licit tubal abortion, even though it might be medically possible to remove the fetus while leaving the tube intact. According to *Ethical and Religious Directives for Catholic Health Facilities* (1971:section 16):

> In extrauterine pregnancy the dangerously affected part of the mother (e.g., cervix, ovary, or fallopian tube) may be removed, even though fetal death is foreseen, provided that: (a) the affected part is presumed already to be so damaged and dangerously affected as to warrant its removal, and that (b) *the operation is not just a separation of the embryo or fetus from its site within the part* (which would be a direct abortion from a uterine appendage), and that (c) the operation cannot be postponed without notably increasing the danger to the mother. (My italics)

Moreover, the directives require that the uterine appendage be "so damaged and dangerously affected as to warrant its removal." By this time it should be apparent why a physician might have to delay surgically treating an ectopic pregnancy. Once sufficient damage has been done to the uterine appendage (by the fetus, of course) the condition of the appendage is life-threatening in itself. Only at that point can the operation be described as a medical procedure indicated by the dangerous condition of the organ itself.[21]

46. On this interpretation of the Principle of Double Effect, it should also be clear why abortion on psychiatric grounds is illicit. There is first of all the requirement of proportionality; whether or not preservation of the pregnant woman's mental health, rather than her physical life, can be commensurate with fetal death. One gains the impression, in the context of Catholic discussions of abortion, that no good except the preservation of the life of one human being can be considered proportional to another human being's death. (On the other hand, in the context of war Catholic moralists have allowed other values, such as the defense of property or a way of life, to be commensurate with the death of innocent human beings.) Even if the preservation of the woman's mental health were to be treated as proportional to the death of the fetus, however, it is doubtful that any abortion for psychiatric reasons could be considered indirect.[22]

To be indirect, the abortion would have to occur as a result of a procedure which would be indicated were similar symptoms of mental distress to appear in a non-pregnant woman. If drugs used in treating psychiatric disorders are also abortifacient, then their use on a mentally disturbed pregnant woman would constitute an indirect abortion. The vast majority of abortions performed on psychiatric grounds, however, clearly falls outside this category. By no stretch of the imagination can the administration of prostaglandins, or the performance of vacuum aspirations, saline abortions and hysterotomies, be considered standard psychiatric treatment for non-pregnant women.

47. Summarizing then: Abortionists who follow Catholic manuals of medical ethics control hemorrhaging or remove cancerous uteruses and diseased fallopian tubes; the gynecologist of Häring's account should have removed a hemorrhaging uterus. Ignored in this accounting of what the physician does is the fact that in each case he deliberately kills what is, on Catholic doctrine, one of his patients and an innocent human being. At this point it is difficult to suppress the suspicion that a necessary condition of licit killing in Catholic moral theology is that it be possible to represent the fatal act as something other than killing. By requiring that therapeutic abortions satisfy condition (1'), Catholic doctrine insures that what the surgeon does be describable as a completely innocuous procedure necessitated by conditions unrelated to pregnancy. Such moralizing exploits the variety of descriptions by which it is always possible to refer to one and the same set of events, ignoring the fact that any and all therapeutic abortions could equally well be described as an attempt to save life or as a destruction of innocent human life.

To conclude this chapter: We have described the orthodox Roman Catholic doctrine which forbids some therapeutic abortions while permitting others, and have examined the important Principle of Double Effect with reference to which this doctrine is justified. It was shown that all therapeutic abortions satisfy the 2nd and 4th conditions of the Double Effect Principle.

Condition (3), which distinguishes among acts according to whether their evil effects are a means to the good end or are only foreseen consequences, is the key to many applications of the Double Effect Principle. It was argued, however, that the doctrine of therapeutic abortion cannot be accounted for by reference to the means/foresight distinction. In no therapeutic abortion is fetal death aimed at as a means. Additional formulations of the distinction between licit and illicit killing found in papal documents and the writings of moral theologians were rejected as irreconcilable with the doctrine of therapeutic abortion.

Our investigation revealed, however, that the moral judgments made concerning therapeutic abortion may be understood in terms of the standard/non-standard procedures distinction. That is, licit therapeutic abortions involve the use of medical procedures indicated by life-threatening conditions whose occurrence in non-pregnant women requires similar treatment; illicit therapeutic abortions do not.

Moreover, therapeutic abortions involving standard procedures may be construed as satisfying condition (1) of the Double Effect Principle, while those involving non-standard procedures may be construed as violating that condition.

Finally, it was suggested that the standard/non-standard procedures distinction is without moral relevance. Consequently, it would appear that the orthodox Roman Catholic doctrine of therapeutic abortion is internally inconsistent.

NOTES

[1] These cases are intended to be medically accurate. However, the reader should be alerted to the fact that there are aspects of the cases concerning which medical authorities themselves disagree.

[2] Treatment of invasive cancer of the cervix complicated by pregnancy is discussed in Lapid *et al.* (1965). Three alternative therapies—hysterectomy, irradiation, and irradiation combined with hysterotomy—are outlined for women in the first or second trimester of pregnancy, and each is described as fatal to the fetus. The authors state that in most cases the cancer does not disturb the course of gestation. The opinion that it is very unlikely that the cancer would have adverse effects upon the fetus was confirmed in conversation with Dr. John Josimovich, Professor of Obstetrics and Gynecology at the University of Pittsburgh. Dr. Josimovich also remarked that death of the woman prior to viability of the fetus was unlikely with this variety of slow-growing cancer.

[3] Tubal pregnancy accounts for the vast majority of ectopic pregnancies (Willson *et al.*, 1975:202). Fetal mortality is nearly 100% (Gompel and Silverburg, 1969:388; Woodruff and Pauerstein, 1969:196). The profuse hemorrhage and shock associated especially with tubal rupture is a life-threatening situation for the woman requiring emergency care given with the utmost dispatch (Greenhill and Friedman, 1974:359).

[4] Dack *et al.* (1965:52) places the fetal mortality rate at close to 100%, due to placental dysfunction and increased incidence of preeclampsia (hypertensive disorder peculiar to pregnancy). See also Willson *et al.* (1975:198).

⁵The extremely slight chance of salvaging a live fetus from a woman who died in an obstructed labor is confirmed by Dr. John Josimovich, Professor of Obstetrics and Gynecology at the University of Pittsburgh, and by Dr. Thomas Allen, Director of Women's Health Services, Pittsburgh, Pa. It should be noted that craniotomy has been superseded by cesarian section. With the exception of the presence of hydrocephalus (enlargement of the fetal head caused by excessive cerebrospinal fluid), craniotomy on a living fetus is virtually obsolete (Hellman *et al.*, 1971:1140-41). That such operations were performed in the past, however, is indicated by pronouncements concerning craniotomy issued by the Holy Office in 1884 and 1889 (Kelly, 1958:69-70). In previous centuries when the maternal mortality rate from cesarian section approached 100% (Danforth, 1966:672), cutting up the fetus was the only means of saving the life of a woman unable to deliver vaginally.

⁶The following Catholic texts of medical ethics were consulted: Healy (1956); Kelly (1958); Kenny (1962); McFadden (1967); Niedermeyer (1961); O'Donnell (1956); Häring (1973). Except for Häring, who explicitly acknowledged his departure from orthodox doctrine, there was unanimity of opinion concerning the four obstetrics cases described above.

⁷A tubal pregnancy may spontaneously abort rather than rupture the fallopian tube. While some spontaneous tubal abortions require emergency care, others (at early stages of pregnancy) occur without symptoms, and the products of conception are absorbed (Woodruff and Pauerstein, 1969:192-4).

⁸Craniotomy should be distinguished from the less drastic procedure of tapping the skull of a hydrocephalic fetus to drain off the excess fluid. Since an intraventricular tap is the same operation which would be performed if the child were born and gave hope of survival, Catholic moralists approve this procedure on a hydrocephalic fetus (McFadden, 1967:192).

⁹One can acquaint oneself with application of the Principle of Double Effect to a variety of moral problems by scanning "Notes on Moral Theology" which have appeared in the Catholic journal *Theological Studies* over the past 20 years, and the texts of medical ethics cited in note 6.

¹⁰While these are the judgments required by standard Catholic doctrine and imposed upon Catholic hospitals by the *Ethical and Religious Directives for Catholic Health Facilities* (1971), it should be acknowledged that in the last decade some Catholic moralists have expressed dissatisfaction with them (See, e.g., Curran, 1970; Häring, 1973). Several writers have undertaken to reexamine the Double Effect Principle, proposing reinterpretations which have the effect of liberalizing traditional judgments concerning therapeutic abortion (Fuchs, 1971; Grisez, 1970a, 1970b; Knauer, 1967; Van der Marck, 1967; Van der Poel, 1968). With the exception of Grisez (whose very modest revision of the Double Effect Principle will be examined in the next chapter), these critics suggest abandonment of condition (3) and the adoption of an underlying ethical theory which is thoroughly teleological. These recent developments in Catholic moral theology will not be considered here because (1) a teleological ethical theory is not, in my opinion, acceptable; and (2) the criticism offered in this chapter of the application of the Double Effect Principle to therapeutic abortion is quite independent of the more general criticism of Double Effect found in recent Catholic literature. For a comprehensive review of that literature, see McCormick (1973).

¹¹This account of the direct/indirect distinction is also invoked in "Declaration on Abortion" (1974:254).

¹²See, e.g., section 29 of the *Ethical and Religious Directives for Catholic Health Facilities* (1971). "It is not euthanasia to give a dying person sedatives and analgesics for the alleviation of pain, when such a measure is judged necessary, even though they may deprive the patient of the use of reason, or shorten his life."

¹³Geddes bases his interpretation of the Principle of Double Effect on a reading of the principle by Anscombe (1961).

¹⁴The Holy Office in 1884 responded negatively to the question of whether or not a craniotomy could be performed to save the life of the mother, where without the operation, *both* mother and child would die. The doctrine has been consistently taught since that time (Grisez, 1970a, 179-80).

¹⁵It is noteworthy that section 12 *defines* abortion as any procedure which has as its sole immediate effect the termination of pregnancy before viability. This definition—encountered

elsewhere in the Catholic literature, but not outside it—appears to be motivated by a desire that the prohibition of abortion be *exceptionless*. Terminations of pre-viable pregnancies which are considered licit in Catholic doctrine—such as removal of a pregnant fallopian tube—are simply not called abortions.

[16]Grisez (1970a:182) refers to this formulation as "what is probably the clearest statement of the concept of *indirect* abortion to be found in the entire Catholic tradition."

[17]The Holy Office is the division of pontifical government entrusted with the doctrine of faith and morals.

[18]A number of such conditions are described in Woodruff and Pauerstein (1969).

[19]A fact not mentioned by Bouscaren is that the placenta may attach to a vital organ such as the liver. Removal of the woman's liver (with the fetus attached) is obviously not a standard medical procedure; it would be fatal to the woman. On the other hand, removal of the fetus while leaving the liver intact is not a standard medical procedure either; it could not be performed on a non-pregnant woman.

[20]"We must wait until the child is viable (at least with the aid of the most modern incubator methods) or until the crisis of dangerous hemorrhage makes intervention necessary, in which case the removal of the fetus is incidental and indirect" (Bouscaren, 1944:165). *Ethical and Religious Directives for Catholic Health Facilities* (1971:section 14) makes a similar point regarding treatment of hemorrhage which occurs before viability: "Procedures that are designed to empty the uterus of a living fetus still effectively attached to the mother are not permitted; procedures designed to stop hemorrhage (as distinguished from those designed precisely to expel the living and attached fetus) are permitted insofar as necessary, even if fetal death is inevitably a side effect." To wait until such procedures may be employed is, of course, to increase the risk of death for the woman.

[21]See, e.g., Healy (1956:224). "It may be that in most cases where an ectopic pregnancy is found, the removal of the tube at once is required to avert existing and grave danger from the mother. But this is not true in all cases. In some few cases at least there is no grave danger to the mother when the ectopic is first discovered. In these few cases the immediate removal of the tube is not licit. The diseased tube may not be excised until it is a source of grave danger to the mother. To excise the tube before this time would indirectly shorten the life of the ectopic fetus without a sufficient reason, and this would be illicit."

[22]Paul Ramsey (1971:17) appears to make the suggestion that Catholic doctrine could consider abortions performed on psychiatric grounds as indirect, and hence permissible, if only psychiatric predictions were more reliable. This suggestion indicates, I believe, a misunderstanding of the manner in which the Double Effect Principle has been applied to therapeutic abortion.

CHAPTER III

Grisez's Revision of
The Double Effect Principle

48. Before leaving the subject of Double Effect and therapeutic abortion it is of interest to examine the contribution made to the discussion by the Roman Catholic moral philosopher, Germain Grisez. In two recent publications, *Abortion: the Myths, the Realities and the Arguments* (1970a) and "Toward a Consistent Natural-Law Ethics of Killing" (1970b), Grisez offers an exhaustive defense of the traditional Roman Catholic position on abortion. Yet he suggests that the Principle of Double Effect be modified to widen the category of indirect killing. Applying this modified Double Effect Principle to abortion, Grisez maintains that abortions performed to save the life of the pregnant woman are morally justified.

This chapter will evaluate Grisez's revision of the Double Effect Principle. Is Grisez successful in expanding the traditional category of permissible abortions, without compromising either the claim that the fetus is a human being, or common intuitions about the circumstances in which it is morally permissible to kill a human being?

49. Adopting the premise that the fetus is a human being, Grisez places the problem of abortion within the larger context of the conditions, if any, under which it is justifiable for one person to kill another. Thus he writes, "killing unborn persons must be evaluated on the same basis we use in evaluating the killing of any other human beings" (1970b:94).

That basis is provided by the Double Effect Principle, which Grisez (1970a:329) formulates as follows:

One may perform an act having two effects, one good and the other bad, if four conditions are fulfilled simultaneously.

(1) The act must not be wrong in itself, even apart from consideration of the bad effects.
(2) The agent's intention must be right.
(3) The evil effect must not be the means to the good effect, for then evil will fall within the scope of one's intention, and evil may not be intended even for the sake of an ulterior good purpose.
(4) There must be a proportionately grave reason for doing such an act, since there is a general obligation to avoid evil so far as possible.

Grisez's modification is to replace condition (3) by the following:

(3') The act must be *indivisible* in its production of the two effects. (This will henceforth be referred to as the *indivisibility requirement*.)

Grisez appears to regard the indivisibility requirement as satisfied where two conditions are met. That is, it must not be possible to achieve the good effect without also producing the bad effect. Moreover, the act must not be divisible into two human acts, the first of which results in the bad effect and the second of which is necessary to achievement of the good effect. Grisez's meaning should become clearer as we consider several applications of the modified Double Effect Principle.

Grisez says that an organ transplant which deprives the donor of life or health is not permissible. This is because the procedure is divisible into two acts: (a) removal of the organ from the donor and (b) transplantation in the recipient's body. The first act, which has the bad effect of deprivation of health, does not itself bring about the good effect of preservation of life. To achieve this, the second act must also take place. As Grisez says, the two acts are not necessarily united; the surgeon may decide not to carry out the implant after removing the donor's organ.

Another application concerns whether or not a woman may commit adultery in order to secure release of her children from a concentration camp. Grisez answers in the negative, as the good effect does not result from her adulterous act alone. An additional act is required, namely the release of the children by the individual who has solicited her sexual favor.

Now consider Grisez's application of the indivisibility requirement to therapeutic abortion. He discusses two cases of therapeutic abortion which are illicit under orthodox Catholic doctrine: the first, an example similar to case C of the preceding chapter, and the second, craniotomy.

By my reformulation of the principle of double effect, some additional operations involving the removable [*sic*] of a nonviable fetus could be justified. An example would be when the pregnancy itself was dangerously overloading an ill mother's heart and kidneys. In such a case, I think the fetus may be removed, because although it will certainly die, the very same act (through a humanly indivisible process) lessens the strain on the mother and contributes to the mother's safety, which alone need be intended by an upright agent.

> Another example would be the crushing of a baby stuck in the birth canal. The very act of crushing and removing the baby, an act in fact destructive of its life, saves the mother from otherwise perhaps inevitable death. (1970b:94)

More generally, Grisez (1970a:340) maintains that abortions having strict medical indications are justified because "the very same act, indivisible as to its behavioral process, has both the good effect of protecting human life and the bad effect of destroying it."

50. Grisez's attempt to place the abortion issue within the framework of a general ethics of killing with application to war, capital punishment, and self-defense is commendable. He does not dismiss lightly the impression of inconsistency or even hypocrisy sometimes given by a religious tradition which justifies self-defense, capital punishment, and certain wars, such as the U.S. effort in Vietnam, while condemning certain therapeutic abortions on the grounds that the taking of human life, even to save another human life, constitutes grave sin.

Grisez himself concludes that capital punishment is unjustifiable. He suggests, while remarking that the facts of the conflict were difficult to assess, that U.S. military force was unjustly applied in Vietnam, and maintains that the traditional Catholic doctrine on therapeutic abortion is too restrictive. These judgments rest on the notion of the inviolability of human life, which according to Grisez may be expressed as an absolute prohibition against directly intending the death of another human being.

In spite of its strength, Grisez's treatment of therapeutic abortion is open to criticism. In the first place, Grisez offers a dubious theoretical justification for adoption of the indivisibility requirement. He claims that condition (3) of the Double Effect Principle—that the bad effect must not be the means to the good effect—has generally been misunderstood by Catholic moralists. They have interpreted this condition to mean that the bad effect cannot cause the good effect. Grisez approves this interpretation where divisible acts are concerned. However, he contends that if an act is *indivisible*, then the bad effect is *not a means* to the good effect even if the two are causally related. More fully,

> My conclusion is that a good which in the order of nature is preceded in the performance by an evil effect need not be regarded as a good end achieved by an evil means, provided that the act is a unity and only the good is within the scope of intention. Means and end in the order of human action do not necessarily correspond to cause and effect in the order of nature, because a means must be an integral human act. If the unity of action is preserved and the intention specifying the action is good, whether the good or evil effect is prior in the order of nature is morally irrelevant. From the ethical point of view, all of the events in the indivisible performance of a unitary human act are equally immediate to the agent; none is prior (a means) to another. (1970b:89-90)

Hence Grisez recommends adoption of the indivisibility requirement because he believes that it is the correct interpretation of the principle that a good end cannot justify a bad means.

It should be noted immediately that Grisez's use of "means" is at variance with ordinary usage. Consider, for example, a person who kills her/himself as the only way to prevent the disclosure of important information under torture. Since the suicidal act is not divisible into one act resulting in death and a subsequent act necessary to achieve the withholding of information, the indivisibility requirement is satisfied. Yet surely in this example death *is* the means to the good end. Indeed, it would appear to be a general principle that two conditions related as cause and effect are also related as means and end, provided that an agent brings about the first in order that the second obtain. Grisez explicitly denies this.

51. Still, it would be unfair to reject Grisez's modification of the Double Effect Principle for the reason that he mistakes the correct application of the word "means." Grisez says he is referring to what is properly regarded as a means *from an ethical point of view.* Perhaps his point can be expressed more candidly as a limited denial of the moral principle that a good end never justifies a bad means (where "means" is used in its accepted sense). Grisez claims, then, that it is morally permissible to use a bad means to a good end provided that the indivisibility requirement, and the other conditions of the Double Effect Principle, are satisfied.

52. A second objection concerns Grisez's application of the indivisibility requirement to therapeutic abortion.[1] Depending upon which of two plausible interpretations of that requirement be adopted, it appears that either *all* therapeutic abortions are morally wrong, or *new* moral discriminations must be drawn among them. In either case, the indivisibility requirement has implications which Grisez would no doubt wish to disavow.

The indivisibility requirement, it will be recalled, specifies that the act must not be divisible into two human acts, the first of which results in the bad effect and the second of which is necessary to achievement of the good effect. Now one assumes that the good and bad effects of a therapeutic abortion are preservation of the woman's life and fetal death, respectively. Consequently, the indivisibility requirement specifies that therapeutic abortion must not be divisible into an act which kills the fetus and a subsequent act which is necessary to preservation of the woman's life. Rather, preservation of the woman's life must result solely from the act which kills the fetus.

However, in all therapeutic abortions the act fatal to the fetus must be supplemented by subsequent acts if the woman's life is to be preserved. Should a surgeon simply remove the fetus of a woman suffering from chronic hypertension but neglect to suture her afterwards or order post-operative care, the woman would in all probability die.

The same is true where craniotomy is performed. Grisez (1970b:94) describes the act in question as "crushing *and* removing the baby" (italics mine), himself suggesting the divisibility of the performance. Craniotomy may in fact be analyzed as two distinct acts: (a) crushing the fetal head (which may itself involve perforation of the head, internal destruction of its contents, and then external compression of the head) and (b) removal of the fetus. (Douglas *et al.,* 1965:478-486). While the first act kills the fetus, the second act is clearly required to preserve the woman's life.

Thus, if one interprets the indivisibility requirement as specifying that therapeutic abortion must not be divisible into an act which kills the fetus and a subsequent act which is necessary to preserve the woman's life, then no therapeutic abortions are permissible. Alternatively, one might interpret the indivisibility requirement less stringently as specifying that therapeutic abortion must not be divisible into an act which kills the fetus and a subsequent act which is necessary to alter the conditions initially endangering the woman's life. That is, alteration of those conditions must result solely from the act which kills the fetus.

On this second interpretation, therapeutic abortion of a woman suffering from hypertension would be permissible. The act which kills her fetus itself relieves her of the strain pregnancy placed upon her heart and kidneys. No additional human act is necessary to bring relief.

There are situations, however, in which the fatal act does not itself correct a life-threatening condition. In a review article on Grisez, Paul Ramsey (1973) introduces two such situations. In a case described by Ramsey as repeatable though rare, a physician can save the life of a pregnant woman with misplaced acute appendicitis only by going directly through the uterus to remove the diseased appendix. That is, the physician must first remove the fetus and then attend to the misplaced appendix before it ruptures. Removal of the fetus kills the fetus but does not itself, of course, alter the condition of the diseased appendix.

Another example involves aneurysm of the aorta which weakens the aortal wall in such a way that it balloons out behind the uterus. Before the physician can take life-saving action to repair the aorta, he must first remove the fetus. Again, removal of the fetus does not itself alter the life threatening condition of the aorta. For that, additional human acts are necessary.

Ramsey contrasts with these two examples the case of a woman with primary pulmonary hypertension who cannot provide enough oxygen for both herself and her fetus. In this case, removal of the fetus kills the fetus and itself increases her dangerously low oxygen supply.

Thus on this second interpretation of the indivisibility requirement, therapeutic abortion is wrong in the first two cases, yet permissible in the third. I concur with Ramsey that it is contrary to common sense or intuitive moral judgment to discriminate morally among these three cases. In any event, it would appear to be contrary to Grisez's intent to erect a new set of moral discriminations among therapeutic abortions.

53. A final objection to Grisez may be formulated through consideration of a counterexample to the indivisibility requirement. According to Grisez, it is justifiable for a woman to save the life of her child by placing herself between the child and an attacking animal. This is justifiable, Grisez (1970a:334) says, because "the very performance which is self-destructive also is protective." Now consider a woman who holds her child between the attacking animal and

herself as the only means of protecting *her own life*. Such behavior would appear unjustifiable to some, and it is difficult to believe that Grisez would approve it. Yet it satisfies the indivisibility requirement. It may be justified by the same formula which Grisez uses to justify therapeutic abortions, namely, that the very act which destroys the child's life protects the woman's.

By parity of reasoning, if the fetus' life could be protected only by means of an indivisible act which destroys the woman's, it would be permissible to do so. In the following remarks, Grisez (1970b:94) does appear to recognize this as an implication of his theory:

> The very act of crushing and removing the baby, an act in fact destructive of its life, saves the mother from otherwise perhaps inevitable death. *On the same principle, one would be equally justified in cutting away the mother to rescue the baby.* (Italics added)

It is interesting to note that except for the single instance cited above, Grisez provides examples in which a woman sacrifices herself for her *born* child, and her *unborn* child for herself. This might indicate Grisez's reluctance to treat the life of the fetus on a par with that of an adult. Elsewhere Grisez explicitly affirms the premise that from conception onwards the fetus is a person whose right to life is equal to that of any person. Be that as it may, in Grisez's account it seems clear that a woman may justifiably protect herself by exposing her child to an animal attack. Since such an act would be morally unacceptable to Catholics and many non-Catholics alike, Grisez's modification of the Principle of Double Effect fails, and with it his attempted justification of therapeutic abortion.

54. To summarize this discussion: Grisez contends that the third condition of the Double Effect Principle—that the bad effect not be a means to the good effect—is fulfilled when the act is indivisible in its production of good and bad effects. Moreover, Grisez claims that the Double Effect Principle, so understood, permits all therapeutic abortions.

This analysis is open to several objections. In the first place, if "means" be used in its ordinary sense, Grisez is mistaken that a bad effect cannot be a means to a good effect when the act is indivisible. Consequently, it was suggested that Grisez be construed as modifying the Double Effect Principle to permit use of a bad means provided the act be indivisible.

In the second place, it would appear that Grisez errs in application of his modified Double Effect Principle to therapeutic abortion. Depending upon which of two plausible interpretations of the indivisibility requirement be adopted, either all therapeutic abortions are morally wrong, or new moral discriminations must be drawn among them. In either case, Grisez's reformulation fails to liberalize the Roman Catholic position on therapeutic abortion, and has implications which Grisez himself probably would not accept.

Finally, the modified Double Effect Principle is open to a damaging counterexample. It would permit a woman to protect her own life by forcing her child to stand between herself and a charging animal.

We may conclude, therefore, that Grisez is unsuccessful in providing a basis within traditional Roman Catholic moral theology for a liberalized doctrine of therapeutic abortion.

NOTES

[1]It may be noted that Grisez believes that condition (3), as generally understood, accounts for the orthodox doctrine of therapeutic abortion. If the argument of the preceding chapter is correct, this belief is mistaken. In no therapeutic abortion is fetal death the means (in the usual sense of "means") to the desired end. Grisez himself appears to recognize this, yet asserts that most therapeutic abortions violate condition (3). In what follows, we shall adopt Grisez's assumption that all therapeutic abortions satisfy the other conditions of the Double Effect Principle. This will enable us to focus attention on the implications of the indivisibility requirement.

CHAPTER IV

Abortion Following Rape:
Thomson's Defense of Abortion

55. It has been argued in preceding chapters that it is not possible to use the traditional Principle of Double Effect to make morally relevant distinctions among therapeutic abortions. Thus insofar as the official Roman Catholic doctrine permits some therapeutic abortions while forbidding others, it would appear to be internally inconsistent.

Grisez's reformulation of the Double Effect Principle which was intended to expand the traditional category of licit therapeutic abortions, has also been found to be unsatisfactory. Still, I contend that it *is* possible to justify all therapeutic abortions. In this and the following chapter I argue for the conclusion that therapeutic abortions, as well as abortions aimed at terminating a woman's support of a fetus resulting from rape, are morally permissible.

My method of argumentation is analogical. I argue that since it is morally permissible in some situations to kill innocent post-natal human beings, it cannot be wrong, in similar situations, to kill fetuses. In their critique of abortion, Roman Catholic moralists frequently construct analogies between post and pre-natal life. They contend that their doctrine provides no more protection for fetal life than a non-religious ethic of killing common to many members of American society provides for the already born. I believe this contention to be mistaken. In my view, Roman Catholic doctrine confers *greater* protection upon fetal life in the cases of life-threatening pregnancies and pregnancies resulting from rape, than would be extended to post-natal human life in similar circumstances.

49

The examples constructed in this and the following chapter duplicate a feature of pregnancy which is absent from analogies constructed by Roman Catholic moralists: namely, that the fetus is dependent for its life upon a physical connection to the woman's body. To my knowledge, the philosopher Judith Jarvis Thomson (1971, 1973) is the first writer to explore the implications of this fact, while allowing that the fetus is a human being. Thomson assumes this premise, as I do, for the purpose of argument. Since her essay lends itself most easily to a discussion of rape, we will begin there. This chapter presents an argument for the permissibility of abortion of pregnancies resulting from rape, and the next chapter presents an argument for the permissibility of therapeutic abortion.

56. Thomson (1971:48 9)[1] presents the following striking example, intended to be analogous to certain instances of pregnancy.

> You wake up in the morning and find yourself back to back in bed with an unconscious violinist. A famous unconscious violinist. He has been found to have a fatal kidney ailment, and the Society of Music Lovers has canvassed all the available medical records and found that you alone have the right blood type to help. They have therefore kidnapped you, and last night the violinist's circulatory system was plugged into yours, so that your kidneys can be used to extract poisons from his blood as well as your own. The director of the hospital now tells you, "Look, we're sorry the Society of Music Lovers did this to you—we would never have permitted it if we had known. But still, they did it, and the violinist now is plugged into you. To unplug you would be to kill him. But never mind, it's only for nine months. By then he will have recovered from his ailment, and can safely be unplugged from you."

An argument given by the hospital director against unplugging the violinist is meant to be parallel to the Roman Catholic argument against abortion:

> All persons have a right to life, and violinists are persons. Granted you have a right to decide what happens in and to your body, but a person's right to life outweighs your right to decide what happens in and to your body. (49)

57. Thomson imagines—rightly, I believe—that her readers will find the argument of the hospital director outrageous.[2] Although it might be a great kindness to remain attached to the violinist, you[3] do not do what is morally wrong, she says, if you reach around and disconnect the violinist. Nor does anyone else who disconnects you at your request do wrong. That the violinist has a right to life entitles neither him nor anyone acting on his behalf to preserve that life through the use of your kidneys and circulatory system without your consent.

Note that the violinist is himself innocent: being unconscious, he did not participate in the kidnapping, and we shall assume that he at no time participated in or was aware of the planning for your abduction. Since it is not required morally that you remain connected to him, once having been forcibly connected, and since disconnecting the violinist kills him, it follows that there are circumstances in which it is morally permissible to kill an innocent human being.

In characterizing the hospital director's argument as outrageous, Thomson suggests that not even Roman Catholics could deny the moral permissibility of disconnecting the violinist. This is speculative, of course: One can only guess what the Roman Catholic response would be.[4] As Thomson's example is hypothetical and original, one cannot expect to find it treated in Roman Catholic medical ethics texts. In any event, a judgment by Roman Catholic moralists that you may not disconnect yourself would be in conflict with the strong moral intuitions of others. And so, if Thomson's example is truly analogous to pregnancies resulting from rape, this conflict would undermine the Roman Catholic claim that their judgment that a raped woman may not have an abortion reflects common moral values concerning the protection due human beings.

58. Thomson claims that at the least she has established the moral permissibility of aborting a woman whose pregnancy results from rape. In support of her claim, the following similarities between the two cases may be cited. In the first place, both involve situations in which one human being provides bodily life-support to what is, by hypothesis, another human being. Just as the violinist has a physical connection to certain organs of your body, so the fetus is physically connected to the woman's uterus through the placenta. As a result of this physical connection, the body of the life-support donor performs certain life-maintaining functions for the body of the recipient. Your circulatory system extracts poisons from the violinist's blood. The pregnant woman's circulatory system supplies nutrients to the fetus and carries away its waste. In the second place, termination of this connection, in either case, would kill the recipient of life-support, while the donor would continue to live. In the third place, the violinist and, by hypothesis, the fetus, are innocent persons with a right to life. In the fourth place, the burden upon the donor of life-support is temporary. At the end of nine months, both the violinist and the fetus will be able to live without this support. Finally, in neither case does the donor of life-support willingly undertake to provide such support.

59. There is a difference, however, between rape and the violinist case. In the case of rape, the fetus develops from an ovum produced by the woman who subsequently carries the fetus. You, on the other hand, do not have a similar genetic relationship to the violinist. Is this relevant? To answer that question, we may construct another obstetrics example analogous to the violinist case, and then introduce the factor of genetic relationship.

60. The following fiction makes use of the fact that scientists are now able to fertilize ova in test tubes, and sustain the conception *in vitro* up until the implantation stage, but not beyond.

Let us assume that a doctor who has carried out a successful fertilization *in vitro* is anxious to know whether or not it is possible to implant the blastocyst in a uterus and have it come to term as a normal infant.[5] Let us suppose that just when the test-tube fetus must be implanted or die, the doctor is called upon to perform emergency abdominal surgery for a female patient. Without gaining her consent, the doctor seizes upon the opportunity to implant the *in vitro* conception in her uterus. Upon waking, the woman is informed of what has transpired. The hospital director tells her:

> Look, we're sorry your doctor did this to you—we would never have permitted it if we had known. But still, s/he did it, and the fetus now is implanted in your uterus. To remove it would be to kill the fetus. But never mind, it's only for nine months. By then we can safely deliver the baby. We can't do anything prior to viability, however, for the fetus is a person, and a person's right to life outweighs your right to decide what happens in and to your body.

The argument of the hospital director is as outrageous with regard to the forcibly implanted blastocyst as with regard to the forcibly connected violinist. Surely it is as permissible for the woman to terminate the life-support she provides the blastocyst as it is permissible for you to disconnect the violinist. Just as you may kill the violinist, so also she may kill the blastocyst. If she acts immediately she can do it herself by means of medication which will induce her menstrual flow. If she waits, the procedure will not be as simple as disconnecting the violinist, and she will require professional care. This doesn't alter the situation, however, for if it is morally permissible for her to release herself, it is morally permissible for a third party to release her at her request. It would have been morally permissible for someone else to disconnect *you*, if for some reason you had been unable to disconnect. (I am not making the general claim that whatever one may do for her/himself, another may do for her/him. If, however, Y is physically unable to extricate her/himself from a situation in which X is making use of something of Y's which Y is not morally obligated to provide for X, and does not wish to provide for X, then surely it is permissible for someone else who knows this to take whatever steps Y could permissibly take to rectify the situation.)

Now let us vary this example by introducing the factor of genetic relationship. Imagine this time that the research scientist removes a woman's ova and uses them in fertilization experiments, all without her knowledge or consent. The physician seizes upon the opportunity presented by subsequent surgery on this same woman to implant in her uterus an *in vitro* conception developed from her ovum. Is she morally obligated to continue the pregnancy?

In my judgment, the moral situation is unaltered. While her genetic relationship to the fetus might conceivably influence a woman to want to continue the pregnancy, I suggest that it would not so obligate her. Consequently, it would appear that this difference between rape and the case of the violinist—namely, that in the former but not in the latter the recipient of life-support develops from genetic material produced by the donor—is not morally relevant. We may conclude, then, that since it is morally permissible for you to disconnect the violinist, a raped woman may have an abortion.

61. Thomson is correct, then, when she asserts that Roman Catholic doctrine grants more protection to fetuses than would be granted to adult human beings in similar circumstances. A raped woman who is told that it is

morally wrong to have an abortion is being asked to make a greater sacrifice on behalf of fetal life than would be required of her with regard to adult human beings.

Our conclusion that in the case of rape Roman Catholic doctrine treats fetal life as *more* sacred than post-natal life rests upon our treating as morally relevant the fact that the fetus has a parasitical relationship to a woman's body. As mentioned earlier, this fact is ignored by Roman Catholic moralists who defend their condemnation of abortion with reference to analogies involving the killing of physically independent human beings. One reason Catholic moralists overlook the relationship between the fetus and the woman's body may be that those who call attention to it usually regard the fetus as something on the order of an appendix, or a wart, or at least deny its humanity.

The present discussion has attempted to explore the implications of the bodily relationship between fetus and woman while assuming, for the purpose of argument, that the fetus is a human being. Consequently, the morality of abortion has been compared with the morality of fatal termination of bodily life-support in a similar situation involving post-natal life. If the abortion question is posed within this framework, one discovers that it is morally permissible to abort a pregnancy resulting from rape. It would appear, therefore, that Thomson has made a significant advance in moral discourse concerning abortion: transcending the impasse between those who insist on the humanity of the fetus and those who deny it, she has shown that a resolution of the morality of abortion, at least in cases of rape, is possible.

This concludes the presentation of the argument for the conclusion that it is morally permissible to abort a fetus resulting from rape, even on the premise that the fetus is a human being. In the remainder of this chapter, I anticipate four possible objections to that argument. Finally, I suggest that Thomson fails in her attempt to assimilate pregnancies occurring despite contraception to pregnancies resulting from rape.

62. In the first place, it might be objected that terminating fetal life-support is *killing* the fetus whereas disconnecting the violinist is merely *letting the violinist die*. On this basis, one might attempt to reconcile the permissibility of disconnecting the violinist with the impermissibility of abortion following rape.

63. According to the usage of "killing" and "letting die" adopted in this study, both terminating fetal life-support and disconnecting the violinist count as cases of killing. (This usage is fully explained in chapter V, section 89.) It is not incorrect, however, to describe aborting as killing and disconnecting the violinist as letting die. So the question becomes whether or not the distinction marked by this usage is morally relevant.

64. Presumably the difference people have in mind when they want to refer to the one case as letting die, and the other as killing, is this: In the case of the violinist, the violinist would have died had it not been for the efforts of the Society of Music Lovers to secure for him a life-saving connection. In the case

of pregnancy, on the other hand, there is no point at which the Friends of the Fetus act to prevent fetal death by connecting the fetus to the woman's organs. Rather, the physical connection between woman and fetus develops through natural processes activated by the rapist, who was *not* acting on behalf of a dying fetus.

In other words, where life-support has been introduced to *prevent* a person from dying, termination of that support is regarded, by some, as *letting* that person die. Where life-support arises through natural processes, on the other hand, its interruption is regarded as *killing*.

The question is whether or not this difference is a morally relevant one. To address this question, let us consider an instance where supportive measures *are* introduced on behalf of a dying fetus. The physician in the case of the test-tube fetus (see section 60) does indeed introduce a dying fetus into a woman's uterus, and does so in order that the fetus may live. If we adopt the above terminology, then we must describe terminating the life-support of a forcibly implanted test-tube fetus as *letting die*, and terminating the life-support of a fetus resulting from rape as *killing*.

Now it would be highly implausible to maintain that the former was permissible while the latter was not. Whatever moral judgment is appropriate in the two cases, it would seem that they should be judged similarly. In both examples the fetus is innocent, and in neither does the pregnant woman voluntarily undertake to provide fetal life-support. So either abortion is permissible in both cases, or permissible in neither.

Those who raise this objection to Thomson's argument will not of course grant that abortion is permissible in both cases. But if abortion is permissible in neither, and if, as has been argued, abortion of a test-tube fetus is analogous to disconnecting the violinist, then it is wrong to disconnect the violinist. But presumably it has been agreed that the violinist may be disconnected. I conclude that this objection to Thomson's argument is not cogent.

65. The second difficulty is as follows. If it is morally permissible for a woman to abort a fetus resulting from rape, then she cannot have a parental relationship towards the fetus. If she did, she would have an obligation, as all parents in our society have, to support the life of her child. However, after a child resulting from rape is born, the woman to whom it is genetically related is defined as the child's mother.[6] It seems strange that a woman has a maternal relationship to a *born* child resulting from rape, but not to an *unborn* child resulting from rape. Since we are assuming that the fetus is a human being, we cannot account for this by claiming that a maternal relationship involves two human beings, and that the fetus is a human being after but not before birth.

66. Consideration of the manner in which parental relationships are acquired in our society may provide an explanation. I suggest that we are unwilling to assign the duties of parenthood to a person who has neither (1) voluntarily participated in the event(s) producing the child in question, nor (2) voluntarily contracted to perform these duties (adoption), nor (3) had an opportunity, prior to the assignment of such duties, to transfer them to

another party. That a woman can be maternally related to a *born*, but not an *unborn*, child resulting from rape is due to the fact that she normally has the option of releasing the *born* child for adoption.

Before birth, of course, no one else could assume the care of the child for her. After birth, it is physically possible for someone else to do this. It is not the raped woman's genetic relationship to the born child which gives rise to a maternal relationship but the fact of her close physical proximity to an infant she knew would eventually require care that parent surrogates were prepared to provide. If she fails to relinquish responsibility for the infant, then upon its birth she is regarded as having incurred parental obligation.

There may be unusual situations, however, in which there are no parent surrogates willing to assume care of the infant. In such situations, her position remains unchanged by the birth of the child. The option of releasing the child to parent surrogates must be genuinely available before it can be said that in refusing this option, the uterine mother assumes parental responsibility for the child resulting from rape.

The point here is that in our society parental responsibility is not simply thrust upon persons, but related to the performance of, or failure to perform, certain acts. Thus a person has some control over whether or not s/he becomes parentally obligated to another human being. Parental duties are normally associated with voluntary sexual acts. Having foreseen that sexual intercourse might produce a new human being with a variety of dependency needs, the reproductive couple may reasonably be regarded as responsible for satisfying those needs. Parental duties may be acquired, secondarily, through legal adoption, in which the parties agree to perform such duties. In both instances, assignment of parental responsibility is contingent upon voluntary performance of certain acts. In the case of rape, assignment of maternal duties is contingent not upon a voluntary act but upon failure of the pregnant woman to exercise the option of releasing the child. Hence, where this option is not present, for physical or other reasons, the raped woman cannot be regarded as parentally related to the child.

Accordingly, while acknowledging that a woman will normally have a parental relationship to the born child resulting from her rape, we may dismiss the suggestion that she has a parental obligation to continue fetal life-support. (Parental duties will be important in the following chapter, however, when we consider therapeutic abortions which are usually performed on women whose pregnancies result from voluntary intercourse.)

67. The third objection is as follows. If a raped woman may terminate fetal life-support, why cannot a person finding an abandoned infant on her/his doorstep refuse to provide nourishment to that infant? Just as a fetus cannot survive without connection to the circulatory system, so an infant cannot survive without feeding. But surely one must see that an abandoned infant is fed.

The answer to this objection requires that parental duties be distinguished from the general duty to assist another human being in distress. A person finding an infant on her/his doorstep obviously has no parental relationship to the infant. S/he has neither produced the infant by voluntary sexual intercourse, adopted it, nor had the opportunity, prior to the infant's appearance on the doorstep, to arrange for alternative parental care. Nonetheless, the abandoned infant is another human being who will die without minimal care. Knowledge of that fact is sufficient to obligate attention to those needs, perhaps enlisting the assistance of others, until such time as someone else can assume parental responsibility.

This general duty to assist an infant simply because it is a human being is quite distinct from the duties a parent has to her/his child. Parental duties are more stringent than the general duty to assist another human being in distress: they are of greater scope, and greater sacrifice can be required in the discharging of them. As indicated previously, consistent with their greater stringency is the fact that they are acquired by performing, or failing to perform, certain acts.

By contrast, one has a general duty to give minimal assistance to another human being in distress regardless of what one does or does not do. Thus even though one is not parentally related to an infant left on one's doorstep, its humanness gives rise to an obligation to provide at least minimal nutritive care until a parent can be found for it.

The situation described here is not quite parallel to a pregnancy resulting from rape, however, for a raped woman can find no one else to care for the fetus similarly thrust upon her. So it is instructive to imagine that for some reason the person discovering the infant is unable to find anyone to assume its parental responsibility until nine months are up, and that in the interim no one is willing to assist in nourishing the infant. In that event, it does not seem at all unreasonable that the person discovering the infant be morally required to provide its nourishment if doing so will not place unusual hardship on her/him or others for whom s/he is responsible. Here the fact that the infant is a human being, with no other means of sustenance, seems to establish a minimal obligation even though no parental relationship is involved. But then why isn't a woman morally obligated to continue life-support of a fetus resulting from rape, and why isn't it forbidden to disconnect Thomson's famous violinist?

68. We have finally reached a difference in obligations to fetuses resulting from rape and ailing violinists, on the one hand, and to infants on the other, which can be accounted for only by reference to the *special nature of bodily life-support.*

The bodily life-support in question involves a nine-month uninterrupted physical connection between two human beings—a relationship in which the body of one performs functions for the body of the other, but not vice versa. Providing fetal life-support is not something a woman does, like feeding a baby. It is, rather, a state of affairs in which she remains passive while her body is transformed by the requirements of the other body to which she is attached. It is thus experienced as a physical modification, rather than as the performance of a task.

A woman who wishes to be pregnant may experience this intimate intrusion with interest and appreciation (as might some persons connected to the violinist). And a woman whose pregnancy results from voluntary sexual intercourse is parentally obligated to provide this type of life-support. We are unwilling, however, to require a person to surrender bodily integrity solely for the reason that another human being cannot live without a physical connection to that person's body. That is why our quick reaction to the violinist example is that the life-supporter may disconnect her/himself.

The reason, then, that a raped woman may terminate fetal life-support but a person may not refuse basic nourishment to an infant, is that there is a difference between providing bodily life-support and undertaking to feed someone. The former involves an invasion of one's body, while the latter does not. Ordinarily, one may be morally required to feed another, simply because the other is a human being in distress. However, this general obligation to provide minimal assistance to another human being in distress does not require that one be host/ess in a parasitical physical relationship.

69. In turning now to a fourth possible objection to the preceding argument that it is morally permissible for a woman to abort a fetus resulting from rape, the problem of the morality of abortion in rape cases has been construed as a problem of the morality of terminating fetal life-support. It might be objected that some abortion methods cannot be viewed simply as terminating fetal life-support. Unlike disconnecting the violinist, some abortion techniques are themselves fatal to the fetus, quite apart from the fact of terminating fetal life-support.

Dilation and curettage, for example, removes piecemeal the fetus from the woman's body. The fetus dies from wounds inflicted by the surgeon's instrument. Saline abortion also falls into this category. The injected saline solution induces contractions which expel the fetus but usually not before it has died from the effects of the solution.

On the other hand, hysterotomy removes an intact and frequently live fetus from the woman's body, and in this instance the fetus clearly dies from termination of its life-support. The same is true of non-surgical techniques such as use of the morning-after pill and the IUD, which prevent implantation.[7]

We may refer to the former techniques as *destructive* and the latter as *conservative*. It might be objected, then, that the present argument justifies only abortions in which conservative techniques are employed. Yet selection of a medical technique whereby the fetus is killed hardly seems of moral relevance.

70. Indeed it is consistent with the argument presented here to acknowledge that where the fetus is not viable, it need not make any difference, from the moral point of view, whether a conservative or destructive procedure is used. Since a non-viable fetus cannot survive outside the woman's body, fetal death is the invariable result of removal of a non-viable fetus whether by conservative or destructive procedures. Unless a particular destructive procedure differs from a comparable conservative one in terms of

the immediacy of fetal death, the degree of physical suffering of the fetus, or the degree of risk to the woman, it appears to be of no moral significance which procedure is employed. (With persons aware of impending death, the factor of emotional distress would have to be taken into account, but presumably this factor is irrelevant in the case of a fetus.) If, then, there are destructive procedures similar to conservative procedures in all the above respects, it will be morally inconsequential whether a conservative or destructive procedure be chosen for use on a non-viable fetus.

When the fetus is viable, however, death is not inevitably associated with removal of the fetus, and it therefore makes a difference which technique is used. The preceding argument offers no justification for use of a destructive procedure on a fetus known or suspected to be viable, provided there exists a conservative method which doesn't present a substantially greater risk to the woman's health. Nor does this argument justify killing a viable fetus during removal by a conservative method, as a Boston physician was recently convicted for so doing.[8] And of course nothing said here provides justification for killing a fetus after removal from the woman's body.[9]

71. The preceding discussion shows that in abortions performed to relieve a raped woman of the burden of providing bodily life-support, fetal death is sought neither as means nor end. The end is cessation of bodily life-support, and the means is removal of the fetus; where the fetus is non-viable, this results in fetal death. However, many raped women seek abortions precisely in order to bring about fetal death. A woman might wish to eradicate a being who would remind her of the rape, or whose care she is unwilling either to assume or entrust to others. Nothing in the argument of this chapter suggests that it is compatible with the premise of fetal humanity for a raped woman to have an abortion because she wants the fetus dead.[10]

It may be admitted that considerable integrity and sophistication in self-understanding would be required to distinguish between refusal to continue bodily life-support of the fetus and desire for the fetus' death. At present, the distinction has practical application only in the third trimester of pregnancy. If an artificial uterus were developed, however, along with a procedure for safely transferring a fetus from natural to artificial uterus, the distinction would be of greater practical importance. In that event, it would be incompatible with the premise of fetal humanity for a raped woman to terminate her pregnancy by a method which kills the fetus. She could, of course, have the fetus removed and transferred to the artificial uterus. By supposing that an artificial uterus is available at present, a woman might attempt to untangle her motivation for an abortion.

72. Thomson's remarks concerning the obligations of a woman pregnant despite contraception[11] will now be considered. If, she (65) says, a set of parents

have taken all reasonable precautions against having a child, they do not simply by virtue of their biological relationship to the child who comes into existence have a special responsibility for it. They may wish to assume responsibility for it, or they may not wish to. And I am suggesting that if assuming responsibility for it would require large sacrifices, then they may refuse. A Good Samaritan would not refuse—or anyway, a Splendid Samaritan, if the sacrifices that had to be made were enormous. But then so would a Good Samaritan assume responsibility for that violinist. . . .

Thomson's reference to the violinist case makes clear her belief that just as you are not morally obligated to remain connected to the violinist, so a woman who is pregnant despite contraception is not morally obligated to continue fetal life-support. Thus in her view, a woman pregnant despite contraception is no more obligated to continue the pregnancy than a woman whose pregnancy results from rape.

Thomson's contention conflicts with the view presented here. I have suggested that a woman has a parental duty to administer to the needs of a human being conceived through her voluntary intercourse. One foreseeable need, obviously, is for bodily life-support at the fetal stage. Thus, on the assumption that the fetus is a human being, motherhood involves a duty to provide fetal life-support. Contraception merely reduces the likelihood that sexual intercourse will give rise to a new human being requiring bodily life-support. The raped woman, on the other hand, does not voluntarily participate in the act producing a new human being. Consequently, she has no parental duty prior to the child's birth. That Thomson fails to acknowledge this distinction is reflected by the examples briefly presented in defense of her view.

First of all, Thomson observes that the fact of a burglar's entering her house through a window she has opened does not make her partially responsible for the burglar's presence there, even though she opened the window while knowing the habits of burglars. In an obvious allusion to a fetus' right to a woman's body, Thomson says that her having done what enables the burglar's entry does not give the burglar the right to the use of her house. True enough, but surely this example is significantly different from pregnancy resulting from voluntary, though contraceptive, intercourse.

Sexual intercourse does not provide an opportunity exploited by a fetus who slips into a woman's body against her wishes. The presence of the fetus within the woman's body is rather caused by her voluntary participation in sexual intercourse. Moreover, the very existence of the fetus results from that act. Opening the window, on the other hand, does not produce the burglar, nor the burglar's presence within the house, but merely provides an *opportunity* for the burglar to enter.

Thomson goes on to say that if she had installed bars on the window as a safety device, and the burglar got in because of a defective bar, it would be even more absurd to suggest that she was responsible for the burglar's presence. True again, but again the example is irrelevant. Notice here that no act of hers even enables the burglar's entry: it is rather that nothing she does to preve t entry is 100% effective, and this defect in her defense is a *condition* or *circumstance* of the burglar's entering. Again, by contrast, a woman using a contraceptive attempts to prevent conception while voluntarily participating in the very act which, if her precautions fail, will *cause* it.

I conclude that Thomson has not demonstrated that a woman pregnant despite contraception is, like the woman whose pregnancy results from rape, morally justified in aborting. While parental duties are not simply thrust upon persons, neither are they totally contingent upon willingness to assume these duties. That a woman participates voluntarily in the act which produces the fetus is, on the assumption that the fetus is a human being, sufficient grounds for incurring parental obligation to continue fetal life-support.

73. In summary: An entirely new perspective on abortion of pregnancies resulting from rape is gained when one realizes that in pregnancy the fetus, assumed to be a human being, is physically parasitical upon the woman's body. The question of whether or not a raped woman may permissibly abort is then a question of the extent to which one is obligated to make one's own body available for sustaining another human being's life.

Now simply by virtue of a person's humanity, s/he may lay claim to minimal assistance from others in perpetuating her/his life. It would appear, however, that nobody, simply as a human being in need, has claim to the use of another's body. It follows that bodily life-support of the type provided the fetus by a pregnant woman, cannot possibly be required of her simply on the assumption that the fetus is a human being.

Nor can the raped woman be held to the more demanding parental obligation to supply the fetus with the bodily support necessary for life, since she did not participate voluntarily in the act which produced the fetus. Once the moral problem of abortion following rape is conceptualized as that of the *bodily support* one human being owes another, it becomes clear that a raped woman may permissibly have an abortion.

Roman Catholic moralists reach a contradictory conclusion because they disregard the bodily life-support link existing between the raped woman and her fetus. They do not conceptualize abortion of a raped woman as *withdrawal of bodily assistance* provided to another, but as a simple assault on another human being, comparable to mugging or stabbing. Within this misleading conceptual framework, to conclude that a raped woman may not have an abortion makes perfect sense. Roman Catholics can rely on secular support for the view that it is wrong to assault an innocent person whose existence distresses another or others.

As we have seen, however, the question of abortion of a raped woman is properly viewed as a question of the *bodily assistance* one human being owes another. Secular opinion does not support the notion that one human being can be morally required to act as a host/ess organism for another. Neither does Roman Catholic moral theology contain any instance, apart from the abortion question, in which one person is morally required to provide such bodily assistance to another human being.

In fact, the obligation in Catholic moral theology to aid another human being is a distinctly limited obligation. Kelly (1951:553-4), for instance, refers to the Catholic teaching that "one must help a needy neighbor only when it can be done *without proportionate inconvenience* and with a reasonable assurance of success" (Italics added).

Thus I suggest that the Roman Catholic condemnation of abortion of pregnancies resulting from rape is inconsistent with principles of Roman Catholic moral theology, as well as with the respect-for-life principle of secular morality which they claim to articulate.

The following chapter will show that the Roman Catholic position on therapeutic abortion is similarly vitiated by adoption of a misleading conceptual framework. Therapeutic abortion is not a simple assault upon one person in order to save another. Rather, it is the *withdrawal of support where continuance of such support means loss of the supporter's own life.* Hence the morality of therapeutic abortion depends upon whether or not a parent is morally obligated to sacrifice her/his own life in providing life-support for a child. This question of parental sacrifice may be raised regardless of whether or not the life-support in question is bodily. Hence, resolution of the problem of therapeutic abortion does not involve reference to the special nature of bodily life-support, as was the case with the problem of abortion following rape. Nevertheless, both therapeutic abortion and abortion following rape can be viewed as raising the general issue of *assistance* one person may owe another, as parent or as human being.

NOTES

[1]All subsequent quotations from Thomson are from her 1971 article.

[2]If the reader has difficulty with this hypothetical example, I draw her/his attention to an actual case reported by the *Pittsburgh Post Gazette*, January 1, 1976:1, in which an unconscious woman's blood was circulated through the liver of a male patient suffering from irreversible brain damage. The woman's liver failure, judged to be unresponsive to standard medical treatment but potentially reversible, was significantly improved after two days of the cross-circulation procedure.

[3]Thomson's selection of the second person singular gives her example special force for readers of both sexes, and will be followed here.

[4]Neither of the two Roman Catholic reactions to Thomson's example which I have seen in print contested the permissibility of your disconnecting the violinist. (See Finnis, 1973; McCormick, 1974.) Nor did the several Roman Catholics, including an activist in the anti-abortion movement and a priest, to whom I put the question.

[5]In July, 1974, Dr. Bevis of Leeds University in England announced the birth of three normal infants who had been conceived in test tubes and then implanted in the wombs of three women whose diseased or missing fallopian tubes had prevented natural conception (*NY Times*, July 16, 1974:8:3). Dr. Bevis produced no documentation for his claims which, if true, would establish him as the first to achieve a human embryo implant resulting in birth. See David Rorvik, "The Embryo Sweepstakes" (*NY Times Magazine*, Sept. 15, 1974:16+), for a survey of current research.

[6]In Pennsylvania law, both male and female parties to a rape may be required to provide support and maintenance for a born child resulting from rape.

[7]IUDs are also contraceptive.

[8]For a discussion of the legal issues involved in the Edelin case, see Robertson (1974).

[9]A section of the abortion bill passed by the Pennsylvania legislature subsequent to the 1973 Supreme Court decision and sustained over the governor's veto depends upon this distinction between removing a viable fetus and killing it. Section 5 of Senate Bill #1318 directs that every person performing an abortion on a viable fetus "exercise that degree of professional skill, care and diligence to preserve the life and health of the fetus which such person would be required to exercise in order to preserve the life and health of any fetus intended to be born and not aborted and the abortion technique employed shall be that which would provide the best opportunity for the fetus to be aborted alive so long as a different technique would not be necessary in order to preserve the life or health of the mother." On September 4, 1975, a federal court ruled this section unconstitutional on grounds of vagueness of the concept of the age of viability.

[10]Chapter VI will consider the sole instance in which it might be claimed, consistent with the premise that the fetus is a human being, that it is permissible to abort in order that the fetus die: i.e., where the fetus is malformed.

[11]I regard contraception as any method whereby a couple or individual attempts to ensure that sexual intercourse will not result in conception. Thus sterilization, withdrawal, the use of chemical or mechanical devices to prevent conception, and the use of the rhythm method, are all contra-conception.

CHAPTER V

A Defense of Therapeutic Abortion

I. A Modification of the Thomson Example

74. In a variation on the example of you and the famous violinist, Thomson (1971:52) has the hospital director say:

> It's all most distressing, and I deeply sympathize, but you see this is putting an additional strain on your kidneys, and you'll be dead within the month. But you *have* to stay where you are all the same. Because unplugging you would be directly killing an innocent violinist, and that's murder, and that's impermissible.

If anything in the world is true, Thomson says, it is that you do not do what is impermissible when you disconnect yourself from the violinist to save your life. By analogy, then, a woman may abort a fetus resulting from rape in order to save her own life. This is to be expected: if a raped woman may abort where her life is not at stake, surely she may do so where it is.

75. Most therapeutic abortions, however, are not performed on women whose pregnancies result from rape, but on women whose pregnancies result from voluntary intercourse. The question to be considered in this chapter is whether or not therapeutic abortion is morally permissible in the more general circumstance in which a woman has not been raped.

Thomson's example of you and the violinist is of no help in answering this question. It fails to reproduce the parent-child relationship which, on the hypothesis that the fetus is a human being, exists between the pregnant woman and the fetus resulting from voluntary intercourse. We may alter Thomson's example, however, to bring in this factor of parental relationship.

76. Suppose this time that it is your child who is afflicted with the violinist's disease. Suppose, further, that you are the only person available with the needed blood type. Assume that you agree to have your child's blood circulated through your own body for a period of nine months. Complications which couldn't have been predicted beforehand now make it apparent that continuation of this cross-circulation procedure may be incompatible with your own life. (The procedure may itself create a dangerous strain on systems or organs, or remedy of another life-threatening condition may involve terminating the procedure.) Is it morally permissible for you to disconnect yourself from your child, thereby killing the child?

77. To construct an example parallel to life-threatening pregnancy, imagine two situations in which you might find yourself. (1) If the cross-circulation procedure is allowed to continue, your child will survive. (This is similar to case A of chapter II, section 19, the case of the cancerous cervix.) (2) Your child will in all likelihood die regardless of what is done. Here the most you can do by remaining connected, is to extend your child's life by a limited period of time—a few months at best. (This is similar to cases B and C, tubal pregnancy and pregnancy complicated by chronic hypertension. Case D, obstructed labor, presents complexities which are given separate treatment below.)

78. I suggest that in either situation above, it is permissible for you to terminate life-support whose continuance is at the expense of your own life. You may disconnect, even when the child would probably survive if you remained connected. It is understandable, of course, if you cannot bring yourself to do this. Nevertheless, you are not *duty-bound* to self-sacrifice. That you are the child's parent indeed places upon you an obligation to assist the child which is stricter than the general obligation to assist a human being in distress. Still, even as the child's parent you are not obligated to assist her/him to the point of your own death.

The judgment that you may disconnect is even more secure in the situation in which it is very unlikely that the child will survive even if you remain connected. Here the most that could be gained by remaining connected is several additional months of the child's life, and your own life may well be lost. In such situations, it is not even clear that it would be commendable if you remained connected to your child; certainly it is nothing which could be morally required of you.

Moreover, it is permissible for someone else acting at your request to disconnect the child. Your physician, for instance, even if s/he be your child's physician as well, may justifiably accede to your request to be disconnected. That is, a physician may prevent one patient from dying in an unwilling and nonobligatory provision of bodily life-support to another patient, even though the physician has a duty to care for both patients.

79. The judgment that you are not morally obligated to stay connected to your ailing child is implied by what Roman Catholic moralists themselves assert regarding parental obligation.

According to Roman Catholic medical ethics texts, parents are obligated to provide or see to it that their children are provided with all *ordinary* measures of sustaining life. (See, e.g., Healy, 1956:80-83). *Extraordinary* measures, on the other hand, are not obligatory, although it is permissible to use them. Many authors cite Kelly's (1951:550) definition of ordinary means as "all medicines, treatments, and operations, which offer a reasonable hope of benefit and which can be obtained and used without excessive expense, pain, or other inconvenience." Extraordinary measures, on the other hand, are therapies which "cannot be obtained or used without excessive expense, pain, or other inconvenience, or which, if used, would not offer a reasonable hope of benefit."

These definitions admittedly permit varying interpretations as to whether a particular measure is ordinary or extraordinary. In terms of the "inconvenience" to you, however, sharing your circulatory system to the point of your own death must surely be acknowledged as an extraordinary measure for sustaining your child's life. Addressing the problem of extraordinary means as pertains to minors, Healy (1956:86-7) classifies surgery to save the life of an eleven-year-old boy suffering from cancer as extraordinary if it involves a very grave financial burden to the family. If parents may legitimately refuse to assume such financial burden, surely you may refuse a therapeutic connection to your child which involves a sacrifice of your *life*.

It is thus clearly permissible within Roman Catholic medical ethics that you refuse to have your circulatory system connected to your child's. This being granted, it would appear that you may permissibly refuse to continue the cross-circulation procedure, should you learn of life-threatening complications only after the procedure has begun. While the fact that you initially agreed to provide life-support would ordinarily obligate you to meet the expectations of others that you continue, surely the grave consequence to you excuses you from any obligation.

80. It would appear, then, that even Roman Catholic moralists would have to admit that it is morally permissible for you to disconnect from your child, if failure to do so might result in your death. This example is constructed, however, as a parallel to life-threatening pregnancies (with the exception of obstructed labor) in the following respects.

First, a bodily connection exists between what are by hypothesis two innocent human beings in which the body of the one performs certain life-support functions for the body of the other, but not reciprocally. Second, termination of the bodily connection will inevitably result in death of the life-support receiver. Third, continuation of the bodily connection may be incompatible with the life of the life-support supplier. Finally, the life-support supplier is parentally related to the life-support receiver.

In view of these similarities, it would appear that the Roman Catholic doctrine of therapeutic abortion is inconsistent with the doctrine concerning the obligations of parent to child. That is, if Roman Catholic medical ethics permits a parent to safeguard her/his own life rather than continue a cross-circulation procedure which sustains a child's life, then to be consistent a woman should be permitted to safeguard her own life rather than continue fetal life-support. If one is not parentally obligated to remain connected to one's child, then a woman cannot be parentally obligated to carry a life-threatening pregnancy to term. To require a woman to continue a life-threatening pregnancy is to require a sacrifice of her life to her *fetus* which would not be required if the child were *already born.*

This conclusion is offered with the proviso that if the fetus is viable, a conservative procedure must be used for terminating fetal support, unless only the employment of a destructive method is compatible with preservation of the woman's life.[1] The case of obstructed labor deserves special mention in this regard. When labor is obstructed, the size of the birth canal and fetal head do not permit vaginal delivery. Thus the threat to the woman's life arises from the fact that in this final phase of fetal support, her body can neither tolerate nor expel the fetus. Obstructed labor differs from the other cases of life-threatening pregnancy in that termination of support does not inevitably result in fetal death. Support termination is not itself fatal to a viable fetus, and in modern medicine performance of a cesarian section can save the lives of both fetus and woman. Formerly, however, when cesarian section had a stunning maternal mortality rate of nearly 100%, craniotomy was the only means of relieving obstructed labor without killing the woman. Taking account of this fact, we may formulate the following principle to cover this and all other instances of therapeutic abortion. A woman is not parentally obligated to preserve the life of her fetus when continuation of fetal life-support may be incompatible with her own life, and a procedure resulting in fetal death is the only means of terminating support with safety to herself.

81. In summary: It would appear that not only with regard to pregnancy resulting from rape but also with regard to life-threatening pregnancy, Roman Catholic doctrine confers *greater* protection upon fetal life than it confers in similar situations upon post-natal life.

Moreover, it would appear that insofar as Roman Catholic doctrine prohibits any therapeutic abortions, it cannot claim to articulate a common principle of respect for life. That is, one cannot plausibly maintain that there is in this society broad support for the judgment that a parent must provide life-support to a child to the point of the parent's own death. While such parental self-sacrifice may be viewed in this society as heroic, it is not viewed as obligatory. Even persons who might regard such sacrifice as mandatory presumably would not insist that it be legally required. Consequently, Roman Catholic moralists cannot claim that in forbidding certain cases of therapeutic abortion they merely articulate a sanctity-of-life principle held widely in this pluralistic society and properly enforced by law.

II. The Choice Between Killing One Innocent Person Or Letting Another Innocent Person Die

82. It is the conclusion of the preceding section that the Roman Catholic doctrine of therapeutic abortion, insofar as it forbids *any* therapeutic

abortions, is inconsistent both with other judgments of Catholic moral theology and with a secular understanding of the limited self-sacrifice required of parents. This conclusion is made possible by recognizing that in a therapeutic abortion the fetus is killed in terminating life-support the continuance of which is not consonant with the survival of the support person.

In other words, therapeutic abortion is a special type of killing: it consists in the termination of fetal assistance in order to save the woman who supplies this assistance. As such, therapeutic abortion should be carefully distinguished from types of killing which do not consist in the termination of assistance. From the moral point of view, it is critical that this distinction be made. That it is morally permissible to withdraw assistance in order to save one's own life, does not imply that one may, to save one's own life, kill another to whom one is not providing assistance. Conversely, it would be a mistake to infer that certain benefits must be provided others at the cost of one's own life, from the injury which cannot be inflicted on others in order to save one's own life.

Just such an erroneous inference has been made, I submit, by two philosophers who have recently examined the permissibility of therapeutic abortion while assuming for the sake of argument that the fetus is a human being. I refer to Baruch Brody (1975) and Philippa Foot (1971).

It will be noted that every life-threatening pregnancy presents a choice between killing one person, and letting another (or both) person(s) die. Both authors attempt to resolve the issue of therapeutic abortion by addressing the general moral issue of whether it is killing or letting die which is morally preferable in such conflict situations. They conclude that if the fetus is a human being, then therapeutic abortion is immoral in situations in which the fetus could survive if the woman were allowed to die.

83. Brody (1975:16) presents the following example as analogous to some instances of therapeutic abortion.

> (1) By a series of accidents for which no one is to blame, five people in room r_2 will be blown up by a bomb. The only way to prevent the ignition of the bomb is to defuse it be [*sic*] destroying the triggering mechanism that is located in room r_1, but the single person in room r_1 will be destroyed along with the mechanism. If nothing is done, that person in r_1 will survive.

In a second version of this example, the person killed would have died anyway. That is, the bomb due to blow up in sixty seconds will kill the single person in room r_1 as well.

Brody's example, in both its versions, is similar to life-threatening pregnancies in the following respects: it presents an instance in which a choice must be made between killing one person in order to save another or others, or letting the other person or persons die in order to avoid killing the first. Further, in Brody's example the death of the person in room r_1 is not a means to the end sought. It will be recalled that in therapeutic abortion fetal death is not aimed at. The first version of his example is comparable to those obstetrics cases in which the fetus can survive if the woman is allowed to die; the second to those cases in which the fetus will die anyway.

Brody believes that it is morally permissible, in the second version of this example, to kill the person in room r_1, rather than let those in r_2 perish. Since the person in r_1 would have died anyway (within sixty seconds), Brody (1975:22) says that "he whose life is taken loses nothing of significance and is not therefore being treated unfairly." With regard to the first version of his example, on the other hand, Brody claims that it would be unfair to kill the person in room r_1 in order to save the others.

With this and similar examples as a guide, Brody (1975:23) proposes the following moral principle.

> It is permissible to take B's life to save A's life if B is going to die anyway in a relatively short time, taking B's life is the only way of saving A's life, and either (1) taking A's life (or doing anything else) will not save B's life or (2) taking A's life (or doing anything else) will save B's life, but one has, by a fair random method, determined to save A's life rather than B's life.

Brody's formulation is confusing because if B is going to die *anyway*, presumably *nothing* could be done to save B's life, including killing A. The following types of cases should be distinguished:

(1) B will survive if A is allowed to die;
(2) B will die shortly anyway;
(3) B will die unless A's life is taken.

In cases of the third type, B will not survive if A is *allowed to die*. However, B can be saved if A is *killed*.[2] Hence a symmetrical relationship exists between A and B such that either can be saved if the other is killed. Cases of the third type present not two but three alternatives: refrain from killing, thereby allowing both A and B to die; kill A, to prevent B from dying; kill B, to prevent A from dying. It is only with regard to cases of this third type that employment of a random method makes sense.

Observe that in cases of the second type in which B would die anyway, if B is killed s/he loses only the relatively short amount of time s/he has left to live. In cases of the third type, however, B could live a relatively long time if her/his life, rather than A's is saved. True of cases of both types is that if neither A nor B is killed, both will die. Presumably this is the general situation in which Brody thinks it is morally permissible to kill one innocent human being in order to save oneself or others.[3] By further specifying that in cases of the third type a random method be used to determine whether A or B shall be killed, Brody claims to satisfy his basic moral intuition that no person's life should be unfairly exchanged for another's.

The following is presented as a more accurate formulation of Brody's conclusion concerning the situations in which it is morally permissible to kill one person rather than let another or others die.

> It is permissible to kill B to save A where killing B is the only way of saving A and either (1) B is going to die in a relatively short time anyway or (2) killing A (or doing anything else) will save B, but one has, by some fair random method, determined to save A rather than B.

Applying this principle to therapeutic abortion, Brody contends that on the hypothesis that the fetus is a human being, therapeutic abortion is *not* permissible in situations where the fetus would survive if the woman were allowed to die.

84. With regard to the four obstetrics cases presented earlier (chapter II, section 19), application of Brody's principle implies the permissibility of therapeutic abortion in cases B (tubal pregnancy) and C (pregnancy complicated by chronic hypertension) but its impermissibility in case A (cancerous cervix). The fetus will die anyway in cases B and C, but in case A the fetus would survive if the woman were allowed to die.[4]

Application of Brody's principle to case D (obstructed labor) yields the following result. If a woman is permitted to die in obstructed labor, the likelihood of post-mortem delivery of a live infant is slight. In order to save the infant's life, cesarian section must be performed. Formerly, this was tantamount to killing the woman. Thus until recently obstructed labor presented *three* choices: (1) refrain from killing, thereby allowing both woman and fetus to die; (2) kill the fetus (craniotomy) thereby saving the woman; (3) kill the woman (cesarian section) thereby saving the fetus. Consequently, application of Brody's principle implies that depending upon the outcome of a random selection procedure, *either* the fetus *or* the woman may be killed.

85. Now, whether or not one agrees with Brody that it is impermissible to kill the person in r_1 where s/he would survive if the others were allowed to die, moral intuition concerning this example should not be used to decide the morality of therapeutic abortion. The persons in r_2 are not providing life-support to the person in r_1, and it is not the withdrawal of this support which would save them while killing the person in r_1. Hence Brody's example fails to duplicate a morally relevant feature of life-threatening pregnancy.

Similarly, while use of a random procedure may be appropriate in some situations, it is not appropriate in the case of life-threatening pregnancy. If a woman is not obligated to provide fetal life-support to the point of her own death, then surely it is *her* right to decide if an obstructed labor be terminated by a procedure which kills her fetus, or kills her.

86. Philippa Foot discusses the Catholic position on therapeutic abortion using similarly misleading analogies. Her essay contains a wealth of examples, none of which duplicates the life-support link which exists between the fetus and the pregnant woman. Two of her examples follow.

(2) There are five patients in a hospital whose lives could be saved by the manufacture of a certain gas, but this inevitably releases lethal fumes into the room of another patient whom for some reason we are unable to move (1971:38-9).

(3) A fat man leading a party of cavers has become stuck in the mouth of a cave. Flood waters are rising in the cave, and all will drown unless the fat man is blown out of the mouth of the cave with dynamite which the cavers happen to have brought with them (1971:31).

In one version of the cave example, the fat man will be rescued in due course. In a second version, he will die in any case, as his head is in the cave.

Foot says there is no serious conflict of interest in the version where the fat man will perish anyway, and hence it is morally permissible to kill him. It is not permissible to kill him, she says, where he could survive if the others were allowed to die, nor is it permissible to kill the immobilized patient in example (2). Foot believes that in general when faced with a choice between killing one person who would survive if another were allowed to die, or letting the other person die, we must do the latter, although she leaves it open as to whether that principle holds where a great many people are involved. Like Brody, she concludes that on the assumption that therapeutic abortion kills a human being, it is *not* permissible to perform a therapeutic abortion where the fetus would survive if the woman were allowed to die. (Foot differs from Brody only on the point of what to do if both woman and fetus will die if neither is killed, but either will survive if the other is killed. Instead of Brody's random selection procedure, Foot allows one life to be weighed against the other.)

87. Foot criticizes the Catholic view that particular therapeutic abortions are immoral where the fetus will die anyway, as conflicting with the view of most reasonable men.[5] Catholic doctrine on this issue often produces consternation among non-Catholics, who cannot grasp why it is not permissible to save the only life which can be saved. Healy's (1956:196) statement that "It is preferable by far that a million mothers and fetuses perish than that a physician stain his soul with murder" is regarded by some non-Catholics as a particularly insensitive and intransigent expression of a view completely lacking in secular justification.

Yet if we persist in ignoring the life-support link between woman and fetus, it is possible to find flawed analogies to life-threatening pregnancies concerning which we *do* have strong moral intuitions that a person ought not to be saved by killing another, even where the person killed would have died shortly anyway. Consider the following illustration.

(4) Smith and Jones are in the hospital. Smith will in all likelihood die within a relatively short time regardless of what is done for her/him. Jones, on the other hand, could be saved only by immediate transplant of a vital organ. Assume that Smith is the only person available who could serve as an organ donor for Jones.

The physician faced with this situation must choose between removing a vital organ from Smith, thereby killing Smith, or letting Jones die. Surely there is ample secular justification for the judgment that in this instance it would be wrong to kill Smith. It would be wrong to remove one of Smith's organs, whether Jones performed the operation her/himself or someone else did it on Jones's behalf. It is thus not mere Catholic dogmatism which in this case insists that it would be immoral to save the only person who could be saved.

Even if it were certain that Smith would die in a relatively short time anyway (and to make the example comparable to life-threatening pregnancy we must on the contrary assume a minute chance that Smith can survive), it would be wrong to remove one of Smith's organs. Many medical writers outside the Roman Catholic Church are concerned lest *any* decision regarding treatment of a terminal patient be affected by someone else's need for the dying patient's organs. (See, e.g., the discussion by Ramsey, 1970:101-112).

This example casts doubt upon the Foot and Brody principle that it is morally permissible to kill B in order to save A where B will die in a relatively short time anyway. My concern here, however, is not to construct a general account of the morality of killing one innocent person to save another but to demonstrate that when one overlooks the life-support link between woman and fetus, one may plausibly argue that certain or even all therapeutic abortions are immoral. We have seen that Brody and Foot use flawed analogies to argue for the impermissibility of particular therapeutic abortions, once the humanity of the fetus is granted. With an eye exclusively on analogies such as the transplant example, one could plausibly argue that *no* therapeutic abortions are permissible.

88. To sum up this discussion: On the assumption that the fetus is a human being, resolution of the moral problem of therapeutic abortion properly depends upon whether or not one is parentally obligated to sacrifice one's life in providing assistance to one's child.

Performing a therapeutic abortion, however, is *killing the fetus*, whereas not performing a therapeutic abortion is typically[6] a case of *letting the woman die*. As fetal killing, therapeutic abortion is widely perceived as a simple attack upon the fetus, an *interference* with it. Letting the woman die, on the other hand, is clearly a *failure to assist* the woman. Thus a moralist like Foot who contends that we owe others more in terms of *non-interference* than in terms of *assistance*, concludes that where a choice must be made between killing a fetus who would survive if the woman were allowed to die, and letting the woman die, the latter must be chosen. Apparently misled by the word "killing," Foot conceptualizes the moral problem presented by most life-threatening pregnancies as one of choosing between interfering with the fetus and assisting the pregnant woman.

Therapeutic abortion indeed involves an interference with the fetus, but what is interfered with is the *assistance* which the woman has been providing the fetus. From the perspective of the pregnant woman whose life is endangered, the problem is typically one of choosing between assisting herself and continuing to provide assistance to the fetus. From the point of view of a third party, the question is typically whether to assist the woman, or to see to it that she continue to assist the fetus. Thus it is only on a superficial level that life-threatening pregnancy presents a conflict between a duty not to harm and a duty to assist.

I am suggesting, then, that there is confusion in contemporary moral philosophy and in Catholic moral theology concerning the force of the fact that performing a therapeutic abortion is killing the fetus, whereas not performing a therapeutic abortion is typically letting the woman die. The source of this confusion is failure to recognize that therapeutic abortion is a special type of killing. In what follows I suggest a format in which the general question of the circumstances in which it is morally permissible to kill one person rather than let another die can more fruitfully be raised. I do not intend to address that general question myself, except as is necessary to do so with regard to therapeutic abortion.

89. First I will state what I take to be the central distinction between killing a person and letting a person die. There would appear to be no simple principle or set of principles capable of unifying the diverse use of the terms "killing" and "letting die" in ordinary language. One may disapprove of what one describes as letting die (e.g., "Imagine letting her die because she was black and the hospital admitted whites only") and approve of what one describes as killing (e.g., "For heaven's sake, kill him, don't let him suffer so"). Thus the speaker's moral evaluation of a situation does not wholly determine whether "killing" or "letting die" will be used to describe the situation, although as we shall see, moral evaluation frequently influences this choice.

Marking the distinction by appeal to the notion of a sufficient condition might appear promising. In a paradigmatic case of killing, as where a physician administers an air injection to a patient, the physician's act is a sufficient condition of death. As a paradigm of letting die, we may compare a case in which a physician stands passively by a patient afflicted with rabies, knowing full well that administration of a drug in her/his possession would prevent the patient's death yet failing to administer it. In this case the physician's failure to provide medication is not a sufficient condition of the patient's death. It is the rabies plus the physician's omission of medication which is the sufficient condition of death. Thus it might appear that in killing, the physician's behavior is a sufficient condition of death, whereas in letting die this is not so.

This approach, however, has its difficulties. Consider a doctor who administers a drug which s/he knows will be fatal to a particular heart patient, but which would not be fatal to another patient. If a sufficient condition of death is understood as what invariably results in the death of any human being, then the doctor's behavior is not a sufficient condition of the heart patient's death. Yet this is clearly a case in which one would not say that the doctor let the patient die, but rather that the doctor killed the patient.

Perhaps a sufficient condition of death should rather be determined relative to some subclass of which the person who dies is a member. In the example above, for instance, one should say that administration of the drug invariably results in the death of persons having the same heart condition as that particular patient, and that consequently the doctor killed the heart patient by administering it. But then every instance of letting die could be considered killing once the appropriate subclass is specified. Failure to initiate treatment for rabies inevitably results in the death of a person who has contracted the disease. Yet this was our paradigm case of letting die.

I am going to suggest, for the purpose of this study, that the killing/letting die distinction be correlated with the distinction between act and omission. This analysis does not attempt to account for the ordinary usage of the terms "killing" and "letting die," and there may be complex situations to which it is inadequate. It nevertheless enables us to deal with the three types of situations to be discussed here: (1) a person dies as a result of a physician's failure to initiate measures necessary to the person's life; (2) a person dies as a result of a physician's termination of measures necessary to the person's life; (3) a person dies as a result of a physician's initiation of lethal measures. On the above analysis, (1) is clearly letting die, whereas (3) is clearly killing.

Category (2) subdivides into *two* types: (2a) cases where an omission is sufficient to terminate the support measures (e.g., not replacing a depleted oxygen bottle, no longer feeding a malformed infant, discontinuing renal dialysis); (2b) cases where an act is required to terminate support measures (e.g., turning off a respirator, removing a non-viable fetus from a woman's body). Cases falling under (2a) will be regarded here as letting die, since they involve omissions. Fatal terminations of support measures accomplished by an act (2b) are troublesome, since they involve elements from both paradigms. For example, when a respirator is disconnected, an act is performed, as in the paradigmatic case of killing. On the other hand, the act of turning off the respirator terminates a support measure which could have enabled the patient to live. Thus the patient dies in the absence of a needed support measure, as in the paradigmatic case of letting die. It is not surprising that uniformity is lacking in ordinary usage concerning such cases. Since terminations of type (2b) are accomplished by acts rather than omissions, they will be regarded for the purposes of this analysis as killing.

In ordinary usage, the picture is further complicated by the fact that some persons vary their description of life-support termination and failure to initiate life-support, according to their assessment of the patient's life-prospects. Thus withholding penicillin, turning off a respirator, discontinuing intravenous feeding or failing to feed a malformed infant may be regarded in one context as killing, and in another as letting die. This variation in usage appears to reflect the speaker's moral judgment that the patient's life-prospects were so poor in one case that it was justifiable to discontinue or fail to initiate support (the patient is allowed to die), or so good in another that it was not justifiable (the patient is killed).

This is an example of the manner in which moral evaluation influences usage. There are limits, however, to this influence. Even a person who approves morally of the administration of a fatal air injection at the request of a terminally ill patient, will regard this as killing rather than letting die. At this point the act-omission distinction seems to be controlling.

Figure 1 below exhibits the typology just described.

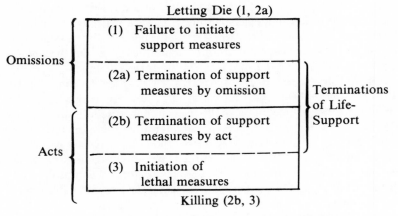

Figure 1. Killing/Letting Die Typology

90. Life-threatening pregnancies typically present situations in which a choice must be made between letting the pregnant woman die and killing the fetus (letting die$_1$ versus killing$_{2b}$). In the putative analogies to life-threatening pregnancy discussed earlier in this chapter, on the other hand, a choice must be made between letting die$_1$ and killing$_3$. Thus none captures the morally relevant fact that in therapeutic abortion (with the exception of craniotomy) the fetus is killed by the withdrawal of needed support. By contrast, we have argued the moral permissibility of all therapeutic abortions by analogy with an example in which a parent makes her/his circulatory system available for a sick child. This analogy properly involves a life-support link between parent and child, and thus presents a choice between letting die$_1$ and killing$_{2b}$.

With Figure 1 before us, we can see more clearly why it is only on a superficial level that life-threatening pregnancy presents a conflict between duty to aid and duty not to harm. The choice it presents is typically a choice between foregoing aid to the pregnant woman (letting die$_1$) and withdrawing support necessary for fetal life (killing$_{2b}$). Since it is the pregnant woman herself who supplies fetal aid, the question is properly whether or not she is parentally obligated to sacrifice her life in providing assistance to her fetus.

Most cases of therapeutic abortion are comparable, morally speaking, to refusing to rescue one's child from a burning house, knowing that one will perish in the rescue. In not entering the burning house, one fails to initiate support measures for one's child. Having a therapeutic abortion is terminating or having a third party terminate support one has been providing one's fetus. In the second case the fatal support is already underway; in the first it is not. In situations where the consequences to the parent of continuing support are less catastrophic, the distinction between terminating and not initiating support might be morally relevant. But this is not the case with life-threatening pregnancy. The fact that not entering the burning house involves an omission—the child is allowed to die—whereas therapeutic abortion involves an act—the fetus is killed—is not morally significant.

91. Case D, obstructed labor, is unique in that it presents the three alternatives of letting both woman and fetus die, killing the fetus (craniotomy), or killing the woman (cesarian section). Moreover, if a craniotomy is performed, fetal death does not result from the withdrawal of necessary support, but from the initiation of lethal force against the fetus' head. Killing the woman by performing a cesarian section is also an instance in which death results from the initiation of lethal measures. Consequently, case D presents the alternatives of letting woman and fetus die$_1$, killing$_3$ the fetus, or killing$_3$ the woman. What gives the woman's life priority is that she is not obligated to provide fetal assistance to the point of her own death. Thus if the only way assistance can be terminated with safety to herself is by measures destructive of the fetus, these measures should be employed unless the woman requests otherwise.

92. In the remainder of this chapter I discuss terminations of life-support of one person in order to prevent another from dying which are similar to but different from therapeutic abortion in interesting ways. I have in mind examples drawn from the problem of scarce life-saving medical resources.

(1) Imagine a hospital with a central oxygen supply being used by two patients, A and B. Suppose the oxygen supply becomes so low that if oxygen therapy is continued for both patients, both will die at the same time. If oxygen therapy is stopped for either one of them, however, that patient's share will be sufficient to keep the other patient alive. Unless one is prepared to argue that where life-saving medical resources are so scarce that not all can survive, none should, it must be acknowledged that therapy may be discontinued for one of the patients. The question of the proper procedure to be used for determining which of the two patients should survive is admittedly more controversial.[7]

By reflecting on two versions of this example, we may ascertain that within the category of terminations of life-support, the distinction between letting die$_{2a}$ and killing$_{2b}$ is of no moral relevance. Imagine that in one situation an omission, such as failing to replace an empty bottle, is sufficient to terminate oxygen therapy. Imagine that in another situation a positive act is required, such as disconnecting a patient from a central oxygen tank. Surely if it is morally permissible to terminate oxygen therapy in the first situation, it is also morally permissible to do so in the second, even though the first is letting die$_{2a}$ and the second is killing$_{2b}$.

In one of its versions, this example of oxygen tank overload resembles the case of obstructed labor in that killing either of two persons will save the other, while if neither is killed both will die. We can also construct examples which resemble other cases of life-threatening pregnancy. (2) A will die regardless of what is done, but if A's oxygen supply is cut off, B can be saved. (3) If B is allowed to die, A will survive. If A's oxygen supply is cut off, on the other hand, B can survive. Substituting the fetus for A and the woman for B, case (2) is similar to life-threatening pregnancy in which the fetus will die anyway, and (3) to those in which the fetus can survive if the woman is allowed to die.

All three examples fail, however, as adequate parallels to life-threatening pregnancies. In the first place, many life-threatening pregnancies do not involve an overloaded life-support system. In the case of a woman with a cancerous cervix, for example, what is being overloaded? The fetus' life depends upon a connection with the woman's circulatory system, and that system is not overloaded. It is rather that the organ through which this connection is effected is diseased and must be removed.

In the second place, and more importantly, there exists no life-support link between A and B in a situation of scarce medical resources, as exists between a woman and her fetus. That is, neither A nor B is supplying life-support to the other (unless one of them owns the oxygen tank). The oxygen supply may be considered a shared resource to which both A and B have access, thereby presenting a distribution problem. It is the woman, on the other hand, who provides life-support to the fetus. Her body, where it in plausible to speak of it in terms of overload, is decidedly not a medical resource which she and the fetus just happen to share. Consequently there can be no question that she is entitled to the full complement of the resources of her own body, when she needs those resources to survive.

Possibly there are those who think of the woman's body as somehow belonging to the fetus, or in its breeding capacity, to her husband or to the human species. It is only the last which could be plausibly maintained, and that only in circumstances in which the species was near extinction, with common weal superseding individual right. Even then it is difficult to comprehend what could be gained by forbidding *therapeutic* abortions.

We have found two distinct situations, then, in which it is permissible to kill one innocent person rather than let another or other persons die. One situation involves the allocation of limited life-saving medical resources. The other involves therapeutic abortion. There may of course be others.

The moral principle which appears to justify termination of life-support in the first situation is that medical resources so scarce that not all can be saved should be allocated so that some are saved. In the second situation the moral principle is that one is not parentally obligated to assist one's child to the point of one's own death.

These moral principles are, of course, not applicable to situations which do not involve scarce medical resources or fatal parental assistance. Hence one cannot infer from this discussion the general permissibility of killing one innocent person rather than letting another innocent person die.

93. In conclusion: Reflection upon the obligations of parents to children suggests that one is not parentally obligated to assist one's child to the point of one's own death. That parental obligation is thus limited appears to be a principle of Catholic moral theology, as well as a principle widely held in our pluralistic society.

Pregnancy, of course, is a state in which a woman provides bodily assistance to a fetus. To require a woman to forego a therapeutic abortion is thus to require her to assist her fetus to the point of her own death. Even on the hypothesis that the fetus is a human being, this cannot, consistent with the principle of limited parental obligation, be morally required of her. Thus it would appear that the Roman Catholic doctrine of therapeutic abortion, in so far as it forbids *any* therapeutic abortions, is inconsistent both with other judgments of Catholic moral theology and with a secular understanding of the limited self-sacrifice required of parents.

A contrary conclusion is reached by philosophers such as Foot and Brody who approach the problem of therapeutic abortion by raising the more general issue of the circumstances in which it is permissible to kill one person in order to save another or others. Their argument fails, however, for none of their putative abortion analogies reproduces the crucial feature of a life-support link between woman and fetus. As a termination of fetal support in order to save the life of the support person, therapeutic abortion must be distinguished from cases of killing which do not consist in termination of support to save the support person. Hence the permissibility of therapeutic abortion, as argued here, implies nothing about the permissibility of killing in the examples presented by Foot and Brody; and if it is immoral to kill in their examples, that is no objection against therapeutic abortion.

NOTES

[1] It will be recalled that a similar proviso was made with regard to the permissibility of abortion of pregnancies resulting from rape.

[2] This third type of case may be illustrated by modifying Brody's example: A bomb is due to go off in 60 seconds, blowing up a person in r_1 and a person in r_2 unless either the triggering mechanism in r_1 or the connecting wires in r_2 are blown up. Doing either of these things will kill the person in that room. If nothing is done, however, both persons will die.

[3] Since Brody formulates his conclusions sometimes in terms of third party interventions to save life and sometimes in terms of self-preservation, I will assume he means them to apply to both.

[4] Brody errs in stating that cases where therapeutic abortion is impermissible arise only at the very end of pregnancy. As pointed out earlier, the chance that the cancer will disturb gestation is slight, yet the woman may die (at some point after delivery) unless the fetus is aborted early in the pregnancy.

[5] It will be recalled that Roman Catholic doctrine forbids therapeutic abortion in the case of a woman suffering from chronic hypertension, although here it is extremely improbable that the fetus could survive anyway (See chapter II, section 19).

[6] Not performing a therapeutic abortion in Case D, obstructed labor, may mean either than the woman (and fetus) is allowed to die, or that the woman is killed and the fetus saved by a cesarian section.

[7] For a discussion of the various selection procedures, together with consideration of the minority view that when not all can be saved, all should perish, see Ramsey (1970:235-275).

CHAPTER VI

Abortion On Fetal Indications

94. Preceding sections have argued that it is morally permissible for a woman to terminate bodily life-support of a fetus resulting from rape, or where continuation of support is incompatible with her own life. Abortion in such circumstances is morally justifiable even though it predictably results in the death of what has been assumed to be a human being. In such abortions, fetal death is not of course aimed at. Hence, the preceding arguments would not justify fetal killing in circumstances in which development of an artificial uterus made possible termination of bodily life-support *without* killing the fetus.

In this section we consider a justification offered for abortion which, if accepted, *would* permit fetal killing even in a technologically advanced age of artificial uteruses. I refer to what is sometimes called the "fetal indication" for abortion, namely, that the fetus is seriously malformed. A woman who seeks an abortion on fetal indications typically terminates fetal life-support because she wants the fetus dead. If an artificial uterus were available, she would not want the fetus transferred to it. For a variety of reasons she feels that it would be better not just that the bodily connection between herself and the fetus be terminated, but that the fetus *die*.

The purpose of this section is to attempt to answer with regard to abortion on fetal indications, questions raised previously with regard to rape and therapeutic abortion; namely, whether or not Roman Catholic doctrine on abortion is consistent with other aspects of Catholic moral theology, and whether or not it properly commands support from secular morality.

As in preceding sections, the structure of my argument is analogical and I assume, for the sake of argument, the human status of the fetus. I argue that the Roman Catholic condemnation of abortion on fetal indications is incompatible with the principle of Roman Catholic medical ethics permitting omission or termination of extraordinary measures for prolonging life. The logical implications of this principle, while disavowed by Roman Catholic moralists, are surprisingly liberal. In fact, they are so liberal that it is quite possible that Roman Catholic moral theology here goes beyond what is generally approved in our secular society.

This last point is a speculative one. Since the principles involved in determining the morality of abortion on fetal indications are much more controversial than those relevant to therapeutic abortion and abortion of pregnancies resulting from rape, it is not possible to specify the relationship between the Roman Catholic position and secular morality with much assurance.

The technique of *amniocentesis*, developed within the last decade, has made possible identification of a fetus as malformed. Available from approximately 16 weeks of pregnancy onwards, amniocentesis consists of injecting a needle through the woman's abdomen into the amniotic sac and withdrawing some of the fluid which surrounds the fetus. This amniotic fluid contains fetal cells, and a chromosomal analysis is capable at present of detecting the presence of all the major chromosomal abnormalities and more than 60 rare biochemical diseases (Powledge, 1976:7). It is anticipated that further development of amniocentesis and other new methods for monitoring fetal development will add to this list. Amniocentesis replaces the statistical knowledge of fetal anomalies available through genetic analyses with the kind of information hitherto possible only at birth.

95. Several reasons might be given for aborting a fetus whose malformities have been detected by amniocentesis. Broadly speaking, the reasons may be social, familial, or fetal. Social reasons include a eugenic concern for the "health" of the gene pool, as well as a concern for the social costs involved in the care, support, and education of a severely handicapped person during her/his lifetime. A familial reason involves concern for the stresses on the particular person or persons to whom the disabled person is related. A "fetal" reason would be concern for the emotional and physical suffering which will be experienced by a person with the chronic, incurable condition detected *in utero*.

I wish to consider the strongest possible case which can be made for abortion on fetal indications. Hence I will not attempt to defend the abortion of a malformed fetus which is performed for social or familial reasons. This simplification will reduce considerably the complexity of the moral issues involved.

In particular, abortion for social or familial reasons involves whether or not an individual's presumed interest in living may justifiably be overridden in the interests of society or the family. If the fetus is aborted because it is believed that it is in an individual's *own* best interests not to live a disabled life, this issue does not arise. The question I wish to address, then, is whether or not it could ever be morally justified to abort a malformed fetus for the fetus' own sake.

96. It is evident that we are confronted here with the question of the morality of *euthanasia*, and of *fetal euthanasia* in particular. Euthanasia will be taken in this study to refer to acts or omissions which result in death, which are aimed at death, and which are motivated primarily by compassion for the person who dies.[1]

Roman Catholic doctrine unequivocally condemns fetal euthanasia. The following passage, taken from an essay on abortion by Congressman Fr. Robert F. Drinan (1973:130) is typical of Roman Catholic opinion.

> But can one logically and realistically claim that a defective nonviable fetus may be destroyed without also conceding the validity of the principle that, at least in some extreme cases, the taking of a life by society may be justified by the convenience or greater overall happiness of the society which takes the life of an innocent but unwanted and troublesome person?
>
> I submit that it is illogical and intellectually dishonest for anyone to advocate as morally permissible the destruction of a defective, nonviable fetus but to deny that this concession is not a fundamental compromise with what is surely one of the moral-legal absolutes of Anglo-American law—the principle that the life of an innocent human being may not be taken away simply because, in the judgment of society, nonlife for this particular individual would be better than life.
>
> It is intellectually dishonest to maintain that a defective, non-viable fetus may be destroyed unless one is also prepared to admit that society has the right to decide that for certain individuals, who have contracted physical and/or mental disabilities, nonexistence is better than existence.

Drinan's remarks against fetal euthanasia are telling in that they conjure up visions of physicians who carry out social policy by administering fatal air injections over the protests of disabled persons who want to go on living. This picture is misleading, however, in several respects.

97. In the first place fetal euthanasia, as defined above, is not carried out *on behalf of* societal interests, but on behalf of the person who would otherwise live with the defects detected *in utero*. Nor is the judgment that nonlife for that person would be better than life a judgment made *by* society. Rather, the judgment is generally made by the person's parents.

98. In the second place, fetal euthanasia never brings about the fetus' death contrary to fetal wishes. Even those who believe that the fetus is a human being must acknowledge that the fetus lacks the capacity to desire life or death.

It is true that fetal euthanasia, since it occurs without the fetus' consent, is nonvoluntary euthanasia. Voluntary euthanasia is defined as euthanasia which occurs with the patient's consent; nonvoluntary euthanasia as that which occurs without that consent. However, some distinctions within this category of nonvoluntary euthanasia are called for. Nonvoluntary euthanasia consists of situations in which (1) the patient is considered competent to give consent and withholds it, wishing to live; (2) the patient is not considered competent to give consent, although capable of wanting to live or to die; (3) the patient is presently incapable of wishing either to live or to die. Within this third category we may make still another distinction. Some persons presently incapable of desiring either to live or to die have nonetheless lived long enough to enable close others to offer a judgment, based on their acquaintance with the patient's personality and values, of what the patient would want. With other presumed persons, such as fetuses, this is of course impossible.

It is important to make these distinctions because objections made to nonvoluntary euthanasia may not be applicable to all varieties of it. In particular, some objections to euthanasia which occurs *contrary* to the patient's wishes are not applicable to euthanasia which occurs *in the absence of such wishes.*

For instance, euthanasia which occurs contrary to a patient's desire to go on living involves overriding the patient's judgment of what will advance her/his own interests, or at the very least involves the greatest frustration of a person's desires imaginable. These objectionable features do not characterize fetal euthanasia. It is possible to maintain that a patient's judgment or desires concerning her/his life or death should not be overridden but that when the patient is incapable of either judgment or desire, someone else should make a judgment on the patient's behalf.[2]

99. In the third place, fetal euthanasia differs from Drinan's depiction in so far as it involves the withdrawal of life-support rather than the initiation of lethal measures. Consequently, abortion on fetal indications should be compared with other situations in which life-support is withdrawn in order to bring about the merciful death of the person receiving such support, where that person is incapable of making any judgments or having any wishes in the matter.

100. In accordance with this discussion, I suggest that fetal euthanasia may appropriately be compared to withdrawal of support from congenitally handicapped newborns. Recent medical literature contains discussions of instances in which treatment was withdrawn from infants born with severe handicaps, because it was believed to be in the infant's own best interests that it die.[3] The similarities with fetal euthanasia are obvious. Infants, like fetuses, are incapable of desires concerning the perpetuation or nonperpetuation of their lives, although if they live they may develop opinions as to what should or should not have been done on their behalf. Furthermore, in the case of both infants and fetuses, it is generally the parents in consultation with medical personnel who decide on behalf of their child that support should be withdrawn.

My strategy here is to set out the Roman Catholic doctrine on the steps which must be taken to preserve life. I shall argue that this doctrine entails the permissibility of a merciful withholding of treatment from infants born with severely deforming and incapacitating conditions, and hence that Roman Catholic moralists should, to be consistent, approve fetal euthanasia.

Roman Catholic doctrine on the measures which must be taken to preserve life is not developed with the rigor and thoroughness that mark Catholic doctrine on therapeutic abortion in particular, and the abortion doctrine in general. I was able to find only one book-length treatment of the subject which compares favorably with the treatment given abortion by Callahan (1970), Grisez (1970a), Granfield (1971), or Huser (1942).[4] However, several basic themes emerge from papal addresses to medical societies, Catholic texts in medical ethics,[5] and articles in Catholic theological journals. Where there is disagreement on significant details, this will be noted.

101. The two basic principles of the Catholic doctrine on the prolongation of life are: (1) Persons are obliged to use *ordinary measures* to preserve their life and health. (2) Persons are not obliged to use *extraordinary measures* except where the preservation of their life or health is required to attain some greater good.

The duties of a physician and relatives of the patient are to provide all ordinary measures of sustaining life, in addition to whatever extraordinary measures are reasonably requested by the patient.[6] In the case of a young child the rule is that the parents are obligated to see to it that the child is provided with all ordinary means of preserving life. Parents may, if they wish, provide extraordinary measures for a child, but they are not obligated to do so. (See, e.g., Healy, 1956:80-90).

These principles are affirmed by papal statement. According to Pope Pius XII (1957b:395-6):

> Natural reason and Christian morals say that man (and whoever is entrusted with the task of taking care of his fellowman) has the right and the duty in case of serious illness to take the necessary treatment for the preservation of life and health. . . .
>
> But normally one is held to use only ordinary means—according to circumstances of persons, places, times, and culture—that is to say, means that do not involve any grave burden for oneself or another. A more strict obligation would be too burdensome for most men and would render the attainment of the higher, more important good too difficult. Life, health, all temporal activities are in fact subordinated to spiritual ends. On the other hand, one is not forbidden to take more than strictly necessary steps to preserve life and health, as long as he does not fail in some more serious duty.

102. The most commonly used definitions of ordinary and extraordinary measures are those formulated by Kelly, and cited earlier in this study. According to Kelly (1951:550) ordinary means are

> all medicines, treatments, and operations, which offer a reasonable hope of benefit and which can be obtained and used without excessive expense, pain, or other inconvenience.

Extraordinary measures, on the other hand, are those

> which cannot be obtained or used without excessive expense, pain, or other inconvenience, or which, if used, would not offer a reasonable hope of benefit.

It may seem strange that a patient should be *required* to use ordinary measures of sustaining life. A patient would normally want to use such measures to prolong life, and where s/he didn't, why shouldn't it be permissible to dispense with them? It is the patient's own death, not someone else's, which would result from omitting such measures.

To answer this question we must refer to the Catholic view that human beings are not the owners but only the stewards of their bodily lives.[7] According to this view, God alone has complete dominion over a person's bodily life. As a good steward of someone else's possession, one may have to submit to the prolongation of a life one would just as soon relinquish. When the hardships involved in the treatments prolonging life become great enough, however, one is mercifully released from the duty of conserving that which belongs ultimately to God. Of course, one may be sufficiently attached to one's own bodily life to be willing to undergo great hardships to preserve it. In that event Roman Catholic doctrine permits one to do so, provided the effort does not detract from the attainment of higher values.

103. Prior to the development of anaesthetics and antibiotics, surgery was frequently very painful as well as dangerous, and classified by Catholic moralists as extraordinary. However, an operation or therapy which today is considered neither very dangerous nor very painful may be considered extraordinary relative to the physical condition of a particular patient.

Healy (1956:64-67) describes an appendectomy, for example, as ordinary if performed on an otherwise healthy patient, but extraordinary if performed on a patient suffering from cancer who has at most three months to live. Similarly, Kelly (1958:130) describes intravenous injections of glucose and digitalis as extraordinary treatment of a 90-year-old comatose and apparently terminally ill patient.

It is evident from these examples that the designation of a treatment as extraordinary involves a *weighing* of the benefits of the treatment against the hardships involved in the treatment. The minimum expense, inconvenience, and pain associated with intravenous feeding will not vary significantly from one patient to another, but the benefit in length of life made possible by intravenous feeding will vary considerably. This distinction between extraordinary and ordinary measures no doubt differs from the distinction made by non-Catholic physicians, who could be expected to describe intravenous therapy as ordinary treatment even where it was expected to prolong the life of a particular patient by only a very short time.[8]

Even where a treatment can be expected to prolong a patient's life for many years, it may be regarded as extraordinary if it deprives the patient of normal functioning. This is indicated by the remarks made by several Roman Catholic moralists concerning amputations or other mutilating surgery.

Sullivan (1949:65), for example, classifies amputation of both arms and both legs as an extraordinary measure. Another moralist, McFadden (1967:253), while acknowledging that modern medicine has greatly reduced the severe physical and psychological hardships of living with an amputated limb, allows that there might be circumstances in which amputation is not obligatory, as where other bodily afflictions make it impossible to develop a facile use of an artificial limb or continue at one's sole means of support. McFadden (1967:255) says that mutilating surgery is also extraordinary in cases where it is possible to "foresee with clarity the truly severe and permanent handicaps which will be the outcome of what might otherwise be called 'successful' surgery." Healy (1956:68-70) makes a similar point concerning a 40-year-old badly deformed and crippled married man who cannot survive unless his leg is amputated. According to Healy, this man is not obligated to undergo surgery. Moreover, because of the added hardship and sacrifice which would be required of his wife should he lose a leg, Healy says the man might rightly judge that he is obliged to forego the operation.

104. It is clear from these examples that the licitness of foregoing measures necessary for life does not apply solely to terminal patients. A patient may be dying, of course, in the sense that s/he will soon be dead unless preventive measures are taken, but not be dying in the stronger sense that s/he will soon be dead despite preventive measures. The patient in Healy's illustration is not dying in this stronger sense. Although he will indeed die unless his leg is amputated, if the amputation is performed he could live presumably another twenty to thirty years.

105. There are two additional aspects of the Roman Catholic doctrine which are important for our purposes. The first is that in application of the two basic principles cited above, Roman Catholic moralists make no moral distinction between failing to initiate extraordinary measures and terminating extraordinary measures. Nor do they distinguish between terminations of extraordinary measures accomplished by omissions, and those requiring the performance of acts. Kelly (1950; 1951; 1958), for example, does not differentiate between what is from the physician's point of view failure to perform a particular operation and discontinuation of intravenous feeding. Pope Pius XII (1957b) in the address quoted above states his approval of the discontinuation of mechanical respiration in certain situations. Shutting off a respirator presumably requires an act. In terms of the typology described in section 89 above, Roman Catholic moralists thus approve letting die_1, letting die_{2a}, and $killing_{2b}$, provided that in each case the measures omitted or terminated are extraordinary. I will speak of the *withholding* of extraordinary measures to cover both the physician's failure to initiate treatment, and termination of treatment by either act or omission.

106. The second aspect of the doctrine which should be emphasized here is this: It is licit to withhold extraordinary measures from a patient without the patient's consent, provided the patient is unable to give consent. Comatose patients, for example, cannot consent to the withholding of treatment, but Catholic medical ethics nonetheless permits extraordinary measures to be withheld from them. The decision to withhold is to be made by a close relative of the patient's, or where no relatives are available, by the patient's physician. In the case of a very young child, the parents are to decide whether or not extraordinary measures will be withheld. Healy (1956:81) states that in making such decisions, the parents are obligated to do "whatever they

prudently think the child would reasonably request if he were actually able to pass judgment on the matter."

107. To make this last point more concrete, consider the following example. Imagine you are told you have developed a disease which will soon claim your life unless you submit to a series of operations and other therapy which will remove or destroy arms, legs, and nerve tissue, leaving you with almost a normal life-expectancy but completely helpless, blind, deaf, subject to uncontrollable spasms, without control over your bodily functions and vulnerable to periods of intractable pain. You recognize that you would not be remiss in your duty to God to prolong your bodily life if you decided to forego such treatment, and for your own part, you would find such an existence intolerable. You therefore decide to forego treatment, even though you know that your death will be an inevitable result.

Since this is the decision you make for yourself, you may in good conscience make a similar decision on behalf of your year-old daughter when informed that she has been stricken with the same disease, and requires similar treatment to survive. You decide it is best to spare her such hardship and suffering, even though you are aware that sparing her will inevitably result in her death. You judge for her, as for yourself, that non-life is better than life accompanied by such travail.

108. Now suppose you are confronted with your newly born infant son who is *delivered* with just those same multiple deformities. Due to exposure to a certain drug during pregnancy, the infant is incurably blind and deaf, has no limbs, and will be subject throughout his life to uncontrollable spasms and periods of intractable pain. The doctor informs you that your son's life expectancy is nevertheless only slightly less than normal. Born prematurely, the infant is presently in an incubator.

You realize that you have found yourself in this situation twice before. Again you make the decision that non-life is better than life. Accordingly you request that your infant be removed from the incubator, to die.

109. Roman Catholic moralists would say that you have acted licitly in the first two instances but not in the third. How is this possible? They cannot maintain that you do not have the right to decide for your newborn that non-life is better than life, because we have seen that Catholic doctrine grants you the right to decide precisely that with regard to your year-old daughter. Nor can they object that in the present case your infant son is *killed* by the *act* of removing him from the incubator, because as we have seen, Roman Catholic doctrine makes no moral discrimination between the termination of supportive measure by act, and the termination of or failure to initiate support which occurs through omission.

What they can do, however, is point out that in the first two cases death is only a *foreseen* consequence of withholding therapy whereas in the last case death is *aimed* at. That is, in the first two cases you do *not* arrange that treatment be withheld *in order that death occur*. Rather, you request that treatment be withheld in order to avoid the use of extraordinary measures. In the third case, however, you *do* arrange that treatment be withheld *in order that death occur.* Unable to avert an intolerable existence except through death, you request that your infant be removed from the incubator *in order that he die.*

110. It is thus the *means/foresight* distinction which accounts for the moral discriminations Roman Catholic moralists would make among these three cases. In the third case, the bad effect (death), is a *means* to the good effect, whereas in the first two cases death is merely a *foreseen* consequence of dispensing with extraordinary measures of life-support.[9]

It will be recalled that the means/foresight distinction, while of no use in understanding the Roman Catholic doctrine of therapeutic abortion, is the key to many applications of the Double Effect Principle. (See chapter II, section 27.) In previous applications, the Double Effect Principle distinguished *acts* in which the bad effect is a means from *acts* in which the bad effect is merely foreseen. Here it is evident that the principle is being used to make similar distinctions among *omissions* as well.

111. It will be further recalled that except in cases of therapeutic abortion, Roman Catholic moralists regard a killing as direct if death is aimed at either as means or end, and as indirect if death is merely foreseen. (See chapter II, section 26.) Hence, except in cases of therapeutic abortion, the direct/indirect distinction is identical to what may be called the *aim/foresight* distinction. It will be observed that the means/foresight distinction is subsumed under the aim/foresight distinction.

112. It is instructive to refer again to Figure 1 on page 74. Striking a vertical line down the middle of the chart, we may distinguish acts or omissions in which death is aimed at either as means or end (left side of chart) from acts or omissions in which death is merely foreseen (right side of chart). The chart is thus divided vertically by the aim/foresight distinction, and horizontally by the killing/letting die distinction. This is done in Figure 2.

Notice that the killing/letting die distinction crosscuts the direct/indirect distinction. Acts and omissions which *aim* at death are *direct* killing and *direct* letting die, respectively. Acts and omissions which merely *foresee* death are *indirect* killing and *indirect* letting die, respectively.

Now, since euthanasia was defined in this study as acts or omissions which result in death, are aimed at death, and are motivated primarily by compassion for the person who dies, it appears on the left side of the chart. Euthanasia may involve the failure to initiate life-support (letting die$_1$), the termination of life-support by omission (letting die), or by act (killing$_{2b}$), or the initiation of lethal measures (killing$_3$). Hence it appears in all four blocks on the left side of the chart. A distinction is sometimes made between *active* or *positive* euthanasia, and *passive* or *negative* euthanasia. The distinction between active and passive euthanasia appears to parallel the distinction between killing and letting die.

Notice that each time euthanasia appears in Figure 2, there is a comparable type of indirect letting die or indirect killing which is approved by

Catholic moral theology. This chapter presents the Catholic doctrine giving approval to the merciful withholding of extraordinary measures of prolonging life. It will be recalled from chapter II that Catholic moral theology approves the compassionate initiation of increased dosages of palliatives which are predictably lethal, provided death is not aimed at but is only foreseen. (See section 27.) This is comparable to an instance of active euthanasia such as mercifully giving a suffering patient an air injection so that s/he may die.

We may now return to the hypothetical examples of your year-old daughter to whose mutilating surgery you refuse consent, and your congenitally deformed infant son whom you order removed from the incubator. Both examples involve the merciful withholding of measures necessary for life, undertaken without the child's consent. However, the former, in which death is merely foreseen, belongs on the right side of Figure 2. The latter, in which death is a means, is a type of euthanasia, and belongs on the left side of Figure 2. It is thus by insisting on the moral relevance of the means/foresight distinction that orthodox Catholic moralists are able to approve the compassionate withholding of support measures, as well as the merciful initiation of lethal doses of palliatives, while condemning the practice of euthanasia in all its forms. [10]

Having said this, I should point out that there are traditional Catholic moralists who *do* give their approval to the withholding of extraordinary measures in order that death might occur. Sullivan is one, and Kelly, somewhat tentatively, another. Sullivan (1949:72) presents the following illustration.

> A cancer patient is in extreme pain and his system has gradually established what physicians call "toleration" of any drug, so that even increased doses give only brief respites from the ever-recurring pain. The attending physician knows that the disease is incurable and that the person is slowly dying, but because of a good heart, it is possible that this agony will continue for several weeks. The physician then remembers that there is one thing he can do to end the suffering. He can cut off intravenous feeding and the patient will surely die. He does this and before the next day the patient is dead.

It is evident that in this case the physician cuts off intravenous feeding in order that the patient die. In thus approving the physician's action in this case, Sullivan clearly condones a cessation of treatment directed at ending a patient's suffering by death. Kelly (1950:219) states that on purely speculative grounds he is in agreement with Sullivan's analysis, but that on practical grounds he hesitates to recommend it lest "the abrupt ceasing to nourish a conscious patient might appear to be a sort of 'Catholic euthanasia' to many who cannot appreciate the fine distinction between omitting an ordinary means and omitting a *useless* ordinary means."

It would appear that Kelly's fears are well-founded. Sullivan has indeed approved an instance of euthanasia. The uselessness of the treatment does not alter the fact that the treatment is terminated in order that the patient die.

It is not entirely clear what Kelly has in mind when he distinguishes here

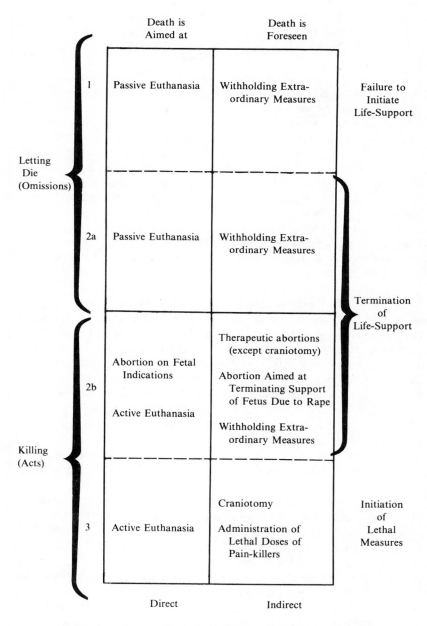

Figure 2. Typology of the Cross-Cutting of the Killing/
Letting Die Distinction by the Aim/Foresight Distinction

between an ordinary means and a useless ordinary means.[11] Most likely he means by useless, a treatment which cannot forestall death for more than a very short period of time. In that case, "Catholic euthanasia" would be available only to those dying in the strong sense of dying discussed in section 104.

113. I submit, however, that even without Kelly's concession Roman Catholic doctrine is committed to the licitness of euthanasia, and to far more than euthanasia of the terminally ill alone. Consider again the examples of your daughter who requires mutilating surgery to live, and your congenitally deformed son in the incubator. What you want in *both* cases is to avoid subjecting your child to an existence so severely burdened that not even God requires that this bodily existence be preserved. If preserving a severely deformed bodily existence were owed to God then you could not in the first case licitly withhold mutilating treatment from your daughter while foreseeing that she would die untreated. In the second case, again your ultimate end is avoidance of a grossly disabled bodily existence. Only here it is not the therapy provided which will create such disabilities for your son. On the contrary, the disabilities are already irremediably present. Consequently, the only way to avoid such an existence is to arrange for your son's death.

Now, I do not see how the avoidance of a handicapped existence can be so desirable an end that it justifies withholding support measures with death as a foreseen result, yet fail to be a desirable enough end to justify withholding support measures in order that death occur. It would of course be immoral to use death as a means in circumstances where the end in view could be accomplished some other way. But this is not the case here. Moreover, it is similarly immoral to adopt a means in which death is a certain foreseen side-effect unless the end in view cannot be accomplished in any other way.

Note that I am not urging the general teleological principle that it is morally justifiable to adopt death as a means where doing so will increase the total good. I contend only that if two acts or omissions are similar in all relevant respects except that in one death is merely a foreseen consequence whereas in the other death is a means, then if the first is morally permissible so is the second.

It should be emphasized that this does not mean that in circumstances in which one is permitted to act or fail to act while foreseeing a person's death, one may also aim at the death of *that same person*. Consider again the parent who withholds mutilating surgery from a child while foreseeing that the child will die untreated. That this is permissible does not imply that the parent may aim at that same child's death as a means. (Similar points have been made with regard to abortion of pregnancies resulting from rape, and therapeutic abortion. A woman who aborts a fetus resulting from rape foresees but may not aim at fetal death. Should her fetus unexpectedly survive the abortion, she may not kill or let the fetus die.) It may be thought that this demonstrates the moral significance of the means/foresight distinction.

We may account for these moral judgments, however, without invoking the means/foresight distinction. The ultimate end of the parent who withholds mutilating surgery while foreseeing the child's death is avoidance of an existence intolerable to the child. The child's death is not, of course, a means to that end. Hence the parent who aims at that same child's death must have some *other* end in view. Perhaps the parent seeks the child's death in order to be rid of unwanted parental duties.

In some situations, then, the means/foresight distinction is associated with a difference which *is* morally relevant, for instance a difference in ultimate ends. This does not, of course, demonstrate that the means/foresight distinction itself possesses moral significance.

The following reflections suggest another reason why some people attribute moral significance to the means/foresight distinction. If a parent withholds mutilating treatment from a child, and the physician is mistaken in believing that the child will die untreated, then nothing is lost. The child lives, and lives without debilitating handicaps. If, on the other hand, a parent withholds treatment from a malformed child in order that the child die, and the physician is mistaken about the irremediability of the child's physical problems, then all is lost. The child could have lived without debilitating handicaps, but now is dead. Some persons may conclude that the fallibility of medical predictions provides a basis for distinguishing acts or omissions in which death is a foreseen result, from acts or omissions in which death is a means.

It would be a mistake, however, to draw this conclusion. The fallibility of medical predictions works both ways. Suppose the doctor is correct in predicting that the child will die without mutilating surgery, but wrong in estimating the severity of the disabilities which would result from the surgery. Or suppose new techniques are on the horizon for enabling persons with such disabilities to lead satisfying lives. Then if a parent withholds mutilating surgery while merely foreseeing death as a result, all is lost. The child could have lived without intolerable handicaps, and now is dead. I conclude that the fallibility of medical predictions does not provide a basis for imputing moral significance to the means/foresight distinction.

114. It is instructive at this point to consider defenses of the means/foresight distinction offered by two Roman Catholic moralists. Consider the following passage from Grisez (1970b:76).

> In this nonutilitarian moral outlook, whether or not another person's death is admitted within the scope of our intention is extremely important. A difference of intention can relate identical behavior in quite different ways to our moral attitude, and to the self being created through our moral attitude. If one intends to kill another, he accepts the identity of killer as an aspect of his moral self. If he is to be a killer through his own self-determination, he must regard himself in any situation as the lord of life and of death. The good of life must be treated as a measurable value, not as an immeasurable dignity. Others' natural attitudes toward their own lives must be regarded as an irrational fact, not as a starting point for reasonable community.

It may be argued, however, that Grisez's criticisms of direct killing are equally applicable to indirect killing.

In the first place, Grisez claims that a person who aims at death accepts the identity of killer and regards himself as the lord of life and death. Is this any less true of a doctor who deliberately administers increased dosages of a palliative to a patient while merely foreseeing the patient's death as an inevitable result? In administering dosages which s/he knows to be fatal, the physician accepts the identity of (compassionate) killer and, at least in this situation, regards her/himself as lady/lord of life.

In the second place, Grisez maintains that a person who aims at death regards life as a measurable value. But surely the permissibility of measuring life against other values is inherent in the fourth condition of the Double Effect Principle, which requires that the good intended be commensurate with the evil foreseen.

That is, the physician who administers increased dosages of a palliative while merely foreseeing that death will result has, in conformity with the Double Effect Principle, judged that the good effect of freedom from pain is commensurate with the bad effect of this particular patient's death. Similarly, a person who decides to forego extraordinary measures of life-support while foreseeing her/his own death as an inevitable result has judged that the value of avoiding burdensome life-support measures outweighs the value of continuation of her/his own life. But to weigh life and death against other values is surely to regard life as a measurable value.

Finally, it should be obvious that the attitudes of others towards their own lives may be taken into account while aiming at death, and disregarded where death is merely a foreseen result.

In a comprehensive and insightful study of the Double Effect Principle, Richard McCormick (1973) tentatively proposes the following modified understanding of the moral relevance of the means/foresight distinction. Both acts in which the bad effect is merely a foreseen consequence and acts in which the bad effect is a means may be justified by their good consequences. This is, of course, a departure from traditional Roman Catholic moral theology which forbids use of a bad means to an end, no matter how good the end. Nonetheless, McCormick does not regard the means/foresight distinction as morally superfluous. He contends that while the immediate consequences of direct and indirect killing are the same, their long-range consequences may be very different. That is, the over-all bad consequences of direct killing may be worse than those of indirect killing. Hence, the teleological assessment of the two may differ.

Why should the long-range consequences of direct killing differ from those of indirect killing? McCormick answers that the person who kills directly is more closely associated with death, more willing that death occur, than one who kills indirectly. This difference in psychological awareness of the bad effect may, in the long run, lead to significantly different consequences.

McCormick provides little elaboration or defense of his view that there is a psychological difference between aiming at death and merely foreseeing death as a result of one's actions. However, his view may derive plausibility from the following reflections.

Consider again the parent who arranges that mutilating surgery be withheld from a child while foreseeing the child's death as a result. Were the child to live without the surgery, the parent presumably would be pleased. This may be contrasted with the example of a parent who arranges that support measures be withheld from a malformed infant in order that the infant die. Were the infant to live without the support measures, the parent presumably would be displeased. Thus it may appear that the parent who merely foresees a child's death as a result of withholding support measures is less willing that death occur than the parent who, in withholding support, aims at a child's death.

Observe, however, that in both instances the parent is willing that death occur *only insofar as death is associated with accomplishment of the end in view.* For a fair comparison, one must imagine the reaction of the parent of the malformed infant were s/he to learn, after support measures had been withheld, of new techniques to ameliorate the infant's disabilities. Were the infant to live without the support measures, presumably this parent too would be pleased. The point is that it would gratify both parents if the good end could be accomplished without bringing about the child's death.

115. I conclude, therefore, that if it is morally permissible for a parent to refuse mutilating surgery for a child while foreseeing that the child will die untreated, then it is morally permissible for a parent to request that a congenitally malformed infant be removed from an incubator in order that the infant die. But the case of the congenitally malformed infant was introduced as a parallel to fetal euthanasia. Hence if a parent may have a malformed infant mercifully removed from an incubator, then a woman may have a malformed fetus mercifully removed from her uterus.

It would appear, then, that the Roman Catholic doctrine of the licitness of withholding extraordinary measures of life-support entails the permissibility of fetal euthanasia. Accordingly, Roman Catholic moralists should approve of abortion on fetal indications where the abortion is performed in the best interests of the fetus. The argument I have presented here for fetal euthanasia may be summarized by a slightly altered version of the passage previously quoted from Drinan:

> It is intellectually dishonest to deny that a defective, nonviable fetus may be destroyed while admitting that parents have the right to decide that for certain very young children who have contracted physical and/or mental disabilities, nonexistence is better than existence.

It must be reiterated that since the moral principles relevant to nonvoluntary euthanasia are much more controversial than those relevant to therapeutic abortion and abortion of pregnancies due to rape, it is not claimed that the Roman Catholic doctrine is without support from a common secular morality concerning the sanctity of life. The claim made here is solely that

Roman Catholic moralists cannot, in keeping with their doctrine of the prolongation of life, condemn abortion on fetal indications.

116. Two questions arise naturally from the foregoing analysis. While they cannot be dealt with here, they suggest directions for future discussion and research.

The first concerns the difference between withholding support from malformed fetuses and infants, and initiating lethal measures against them. Once it is admitted that it is permissible to withhold supportive measures from a defective fetus or infant in order that a merciful death may occur, is there any reason why lethal measures could not be initiated for the same purpose? In his study of the well-publicized Johns Hopkins case in which the parents of a Downs syndrome infant born with an intestinal blockage refused to have the blockage corrected by simple surgery, the Protestant moralist Gustafson (1973:547) raises this question.

> Once a decision is made not to engage in a life-sustaining and lifesaving procedure, has not the crucial corner been turned? If that is a reasonable and moral thing to do, on what grounds would one argue that it is wrong to hasten death?

It might, in fact, be argued that it is sometimes preferable to hasten death rather than to allow death to come naturally. The Downs syndrome infant in this particular case took 15 days to die after all the supportive measures had been withdrawn. The Roman Catholic theologian Maguire (1974:11) points out that "though the death of this child *may* have been merciful, its dying was not," and suggests that this might be a case in which withholding therapy is harder to justify than initiating lethal measures.

The second question is in what circumstances can it truly be said that non-existence is better than existence with certain disabilities? As far as I know, no longitudinal studies have been made of persons born with serious malformities. Do these people wish they had not been born? In the absence of empirical research into the conditions under which a person would prefer not to have lived, we can expect that parental perception of the manner of child it would be pleasing to rear will often fill the void. To combat this tendency, it would be necessary to establish empirically based limits on the range of malformities with reference to which a parent may choose death for a child. Until such limits have been established, a practice of infant and fetal euthanasia cannot seriously be recommended.

NOTES

[1]This characterization of euthanasia is drawn from an unpublished doctoral dissertation on voluntary euthanasia by Bok (1970).

[2]The same point is made by Smith (1974). A similar point is accepted, furthermore, where the use of experimental procedures is at issue. It is not considered proper to use experimental medical procedures on a competent adult without her/his consent. It is considered proper, however, for a parent to consent to the use of such procedures on a child where the parent judges this to be in the child's own best interests. See, e.g., Ramsey (1970:1-58).

[3]A recent article in the *New England Journal of Medicine* describes itself as breaking a taboo of silence by disclosing that in the special care nursery of the Yale-New Haven Hospital from January 1970 to June 1972, there were 43 deaths related to decisions by physicians and parents to withhold treatment from newborns whose "prognosis for meaningful life was extremely poor or hopeless." (Duff and Campbell, 1973). A physician responsible for an English clinic specializing in treatment of babies born with spina bifida argues that the past policy of his clinic to treat all infants is not in the interest of the patients, and urges selective treatment only. (Lorber, 1971, 1973). For additional medical literature, consult Foltz *et al.* (1972) and Shaw (1973). For a discussion by an ethicist of the moral issues involved in the well-publicized Johns Hopkins case in which the parents of a Downs syndrome infant withheld consent to simple corrective surgery, see Gustafson (1973). Additional discussion of ethical issues occurs in Bard and Fletcher, Joseph (1968); Cooke (1972); Fletcher, John (1974); Freeman, E. (1972); Freeman, J. and Cooke (1972); Reich and Smith, H. (1973); Smith, D. (1974); and Zachery (1968).

[4]This is *Death by Choice* (1974), by the theologian Daniel C. Maguire. Maguire argues for the liberalization of the orthodox Catholic doctrine. An exposition of the orthodox doctrine, presently out of print and having little depth, is given by Sullivan (1949).

[5]Texts consulted were: Häring (1973); Healy (1956); Kelly (1958); Kenny (1962); Marshall (1964); McFadden (1967); and O'Donnell (1959).

[6]See, e.g., Kelly (1950:216). Kelly also mentions that the physician's professional ideal may create obligations which extend beyond the duties and wishes of the patient.

[7]For a good exposition of this doctrine, see Häring (1973:66-73).

[8]With regard to glucose and digitalis for a 90-year-old comatose patient, Kelly (1958:130) says that moralists would generally say this was ordinary means if it were merely a matter of tiding a patient over a temporary crisis, yet "in the present case the actual benefit they confer on the patient is so slight in comparison with the continued cost and difficulty of hospitalization and care that their use should be called an *extraordinary* means of preserving life."

[9]Häring (1973:146), for example, writes that he trusts the non-Catholic reader will not consider it "hairsplitting" to distinguish between cases in which the direct objective is to dispense with extraordinary measures and cases where treatment is omitted or stopped in order to allow the patient to die.

[10]Kenny (1962:134), for example, claims that "the proponents of euthanasia have little, if any, conception of morality."

[11]In Kelley's 1951 article, he defines ordinary means as means which, among other things, offers "a reasonable hope of benefit." Thus in this later article he appears to have incorporated the notion of usefulness into his concept of an ordinary means.

CHAPTER VII

Conclusions

This study has, for the sake of argument, granted the Roman Catholic premise that the fetus is a human being. This concession notwithstanding, it is possible to criticize Catholic doctrine. Specifically, the following conclusions have emerged:

1. Insofar as it uses the Principle of Double Effect to permit some therapeutic abortions while forbidding others, the Roman Catholic doctrine of therapeutic abortion is untenable.

2. Insofar as it forbids *any* therapeutic abortions, the Roman Catholic doctrine of therapeutic abortion is inconsistent with a moral principle generally held within our secular society as well as by Catholic moralists themselves concerning the sacrifice parents can be required to make for their children. Hence, the Catholic condemnation of certain therapeutic abortions can claim no support from secular morality and is furthermore inconsistent with other aspects of Catholic moral theology.

3. The Roman Catholic condemnation of abortion of pregnancies resulting from rape is inconsistent with a moral principle generally held within our secular society as well as by Catholic moralists themselves concerning the assistance one human being can be required to render another. Hence, the Catholic condemnation of abortion of pregnancies resulting from rape can claim no support from secular morality and is furthermore inconsistent with other aspects of Catholic moral theology.

4. The Roman Catholic condemnation of abortion on fetal indications is inconsistent with the Catholic moral principle permitting omission or termination of extraordinary measures of prolonging life.

In sum, it can be concluded that the Roman Catholic appeal for restrictive abortion legislation is vitiated by doctrinal inconsistencies and a failure to identify correctly the common moral principles applicable to the problem of abortion.

References

Anscombe, G. E. M.
    1961   "War and murder." Pp. 45-62 in Walter Stein (ed.), *Nuclear Weapons: A Catholic Response*. New York: Sheed and Ward.
Aquinas, Thomas
    1912-25   *Summa Theologica*. London: Burns Oates and Washburn, Ltd.
Augustine
    1955   "The good of marriage." Pp. 9-51 in Roy J. Deferrari (ed.), *The Fathers of the Church*, Vol. 27. New York: Fathers of the Church.
Bard, B., and Fletcher, Joseph
    1968   "The right to die." *Atlantic* (April):59-64.
de Beauvoir, Simone
    1953   *The Second Sex*. Translated and edited by H. M. Parshley. New York: Alfred A. Knopf.
Bennett, Jonathan
    1971   "Whatever the consequences." Pp. 42-66 in James Rachels (ed.), *Moral Problems*. New York: Harper and Row.
Bok, Sissela Ann
    1970   *Voluntary Euthanasia*. Unpublished dissertation. Harvard University.
Bouscaren, T. Lincoln
    1944   *Ethics of Ectopic Operations*, 2nd ed. Milwaukee: Bruce Publishing Co.
Brody, Baruch
    1971   "Abortion and the law." *Journal of Philosophy* 68:357-369.
    1973   "Abortion and the sanctity of human life." *American Philosophical Quarterly* 10:133-140.
    1975   *Abortion and the Sanctity of Human Life: A Philosophical View*. Cambridge, Mass.: MIT Press.
Buckley, James L.
    1974   "Statement of Hon. James L. Buckley." *Abortion—Part I: Hearings Before the Subcommittee on Constitutional Amendments of the Committee on the Judiciary*. Washington: U.S. Government Printing Office.
Byrn, Robert M.
    1973a   "An American tragedy: the Supreme Court on abortion." *Fordham Law Review* 41:807-862.
    1973b   "Goodbye to the Judeo-Christian era in law." *America* 128:511-514.

Callahan, Daniel, ed.
   1969   *The Catholic Case for Contraception*. New York: Macmillan.
Callahan, Daniel
   1970   *Abortion: Law, Choice and Morality*. New York: Macmillan.
Cooke, Robert E.
   1972   "Whose suffering?" *Journal of Pediatrics* 80:906-907.
Curran, Charles E.
   1970   *A New Look at Christian Morality*. Notre Dame, Indiana: Fides Publishers.
   1973   "Abortion: law and morality in contemporary Catholic theology." *Jurist* 33:162-183.
Dack, Simon *et al.*
   1965   "Heart disease." Pp. 1-63 in Joseph J. Rovinsky and Alan F. Guttmacher (eds.), *Medical, Surgical and Gynecologic Complications of Pregnancy*, 2nd. ed. Baltimore: Williams and Wilkins Co.
Daly, Mary
   1968   *The Church and the Second Sex*. New York: Harper and Row.
Danforth, David N., ed.
   1966   *Textbook of Obstetrics and Gynecology*. New York: Harper and Row.
"Declaration on procured abortion"
   1974   Issued by the Sacred Congregation for the Doctrine of the Faith. *The Pope Speaks* 19:250-262.
Dedek, John F.
   1972   *Human Life: Some Moral Issues*. New York: Sheed and Ward.
Documentation on the Right to Life and Abortion
   1974   Washington, D.C.: United States Catholic Conference.
Douglas, R. Gordon *et al.*
   1965   *Operative Obstetrics*, 2nd ed. New York: Appleton-Century-Crofts.
Drinan, Robert F.
   1973   "The inviolability of the right to be born." Pp. 123-138 in David F. Walbert and J. Douglas Butler (eds.), *Abortion, Society and the Law*. Cleveland: The Press of Case Western Reserve University.
Duff, Raymond S., and Campbell, A. G. M.
   1973   "Moral and ethical dilemmas in the special-care nursery." *New England Journal of Medicine* 289:890-894.
Epictetus
   1956   *Enchiridion, and Marcus Aurelius: Meditations*. Chicago: Henry Regnery Co.
Ethical and Religious Directives for Catholic Health Facilities
   1971   Washington, D.C.: Department of Health Affairs, United States Catholic Conference.
Farrahar, Joseph J.
   1963   "Notes on moral theology." *Theological Studies* 24:53-105.
Finnis, John
   1973   "The rights and wrongs of abortion: a reply to Judith Thomson." *Philosophy and Public Affairs* 2:117-145.
Fletcher, John
   1974   "Attitudes towards defective newborns." *Hastings Center Studies* 2:21-32.
Foltz, Eldon L. *et al.*
   1972   "To treat or not to treat: a neurosurgeon's perspective of myelomeningocele." *Clinical Neurosurgery* 20:147-163.
Foot, Philippa
   1971   "The problem of abortion and the doctrine of the double effect." Pp. 28-41 in James Rachels (ed.), *Moral Problems*. New York: Harper and Row.
Freeman, Elaine
   1972   "The God committee." *New York Times Magazine* (May 21, 1972):84-90.

Freeman, John M., and Cooke, Robert E.
    1972   "Is there a right to die—quickly?" *Journal of Pediatrics* 80:904-908.
Fuchs, Joseph
    1971   "The absoluteness of moral terms." *Gregorianum* 52:415-458.
Geddes, Leonard
    1973   "On the intrinsic wrongfulness of killing innocent people." *Analysis* 33:93-97.
Gompel, Claude, and Silverberg, S. G.
    1969   *Pathology in Gynecology and Obstetrics.* Philadelphia: Lippincott and Co.
Granfield, David
    1971   *The Abortion Decision,* rev. ed. New York: Doubleday and Co.
Greenhill, J. P., and Friedman, Emanuel A.
    1974   *Biological Principles and Modern Practice of Obstetrics.* Philadelphia: W. B. Saunders Company.
Grisez, Germain G.
    1970a   *Abortion: The Myths, the Realities, and the Arguments.* New York: Corpus Books.
    1970b   "Toward a consistent natural-law ethics of killing." *American Journal of Jurisprudence* 15:64-96.
Gustafson, James M.
    1973   "Mongolism, parental desires, and the right to life." *Perspectives in Biology and Medicine* 16:529-557.
Häring, Bernard
    1970   "A theological evaluation." Pp. 123-145 in John T. Noonan, Jr. (ed.), *The Morality of Abortion.* Cambridge, Mass.: Harvard University Press.
    1973   *Medical Ethics.* Notre Dame, Indiana: Fides Publishers.
Hart, H. L. A.
    1968   "Intention and punishment." Pp. 113-135 in *Punishment and Responsibility: Essays in the Philosophy of Law.* New York: Oxford University Press.
Healy, Edwin F.
    1956   *Medical Ethics.* Chicago: Loyola University Press.
Hellman, Louis M. *et al.*
    1971   *Williams Obstetrics,* 14th ed. New York: Appleton-Century-Crofts.
Huser, Roger J.
    1942   *The Crime of Abortion in Canon Law.* Washington, D.C.: Catholic University of America Press.
Kelly, Gerald
    1950   "The duty of using artificial means of preserving life." *Theological Studies* 11:203-220.
    1951   "Notes: the duty to preserve life." *Theological Studies* 12:550-556.
    1955   *Medico-Moral Problems,* Part I. St. Louis: The Catholic Hospital Association.
    1958   *Medico-Moral Problems.* St. Louis: The Catholic Hospital Association.
Kenny, John P.
    1962   *Principles of Medical Ethics,* 2nd ed. Westminster, Maryland: The Newman Press.
Knauer, Peter
    1967   "The hermeneutic function of the principle of the double effect." *Natural Law Forum* 12:132-162.
Lapid, Louis S. *et al.*
    1965   "Carcinoma of the cervix." Pp. 349-358 in Joseph J. Rovinsky and Alan F. Guttmacher (eds.), *Medical, Surgical, and Gynecologic Complications of Pregnancy,* 2nd ed. Baltimore: Williams and Wilkins Co.
Lorber, John
    1971   "Results of treatment of myelomeningocele." *Developmental Medicine and Child Neurology* 13:279-303.
    1973   "Early results of selective treatment of spina bifida cystica." *British Medical Journal,* no. 4:201-204.

Maguire, Daniel C.
    1974   *Death by Choice.* Garden City, New York: Doubleday.
Marcus Aurelius
    1956   *Meditations, and Epictetus: Enchiridion.* Chicago: Henry Regnery Co.
Marshall, John
    1964   *Medicine and Morals.* Glen Rock, N.J.: Paulist Press.
McCormick, Richard A.
    1973   *Ambiguity in Moral Choice.* The 1973 Pere Marquette Theology Lecture.
    1974   "Notes on moral theology: the abortion dossier." *Theological Studies* 35:312-359.
McFadden, Charles J.
    1967   *Medical Ethics,* 6th ed. Philadelphia: F. A. Davis.
Micallef, Paul J.
    1972   "Abortion and the principles of legislation." *Laval Theologique et Philosophique*
            28:267-303.
Niedermeyer, Albert
    1961   *Compendium of Pastoral Medicine,* trans. by Fulgence Buonanno. New York:
            Joseph P. Wagner, Inc.
Noonan, John T., Jr.
    1966   *Contraception: A History of Its Treatment by the Catholic Theologians and
            Canonists.* Cambridge, Massachusetts: Harvard University Press.
    1970   "An almost absolute value in history." Pp. 1-59 in John T. Noonan, Jr. (ed.), *The
            Morality of Abortion.* Cambridge, Massachusetts: Harvard University Press.
O'Donnell, Thomas J.
    1959   *Morals in Medicine.* Westminster, Maryland: The Newman Press.
Plato
    1963   *Collected Dialogues.* Edith Hamilton and Huntingdon Cairns (eds.), rev. ed.
            New York: Random House.
Powledge, Tabitha M.
    1976   "From experimental procedure to accepted practice." *Hastings Center Report* 6:6-7.
Ramsey, Paul
    1970   *The Patient as Person: Explorations in Medical Ethics.* New Haven: Yale University
            Press.
    1971   "The morality of abortion." Pp. 3-27 in James Rachels (ed.), *Moral Problems.* New
            York: Harper and Row.
    1973   "Abortion: a review article." *Thomist* 37:174-226.
Reich, Warren T., and Smith, Harmon
    1973   "Case studies in bioethics: on the birth of a severely handicapped infant." *Hastings
            Center Report* 3:10-12.
Robertson, John A.
    1974   "Medical ethics in the courtroom." *Hastings Center Report* 4:1-3.
Shaw, Anthony
    1973   "Dilemmas of 'informed consent' in children." *New England Journal of Medicine*
            289:885-890.
Smith, David H.
    1974   "On letting some babies die." *Hastings Center Studies* 2:37-46.
Sullivan, Joseph V.
    1949   *Catholic Teaching on the Morality of Euthanasia.* Washington, D.C., Catholic
            University of America Press.
Thomson, Judith Jarvis
    1971   "A defense of abortion." *Philosophy and Public Affairs* 1:47-66.
    1973   "Rights and deaths." *Philosophy and Public Affairs* 2:146-159.
Van der Marck, William
    1967   *Toward a Christian Ethic: A Renewal of Moral Theology.* Westminster, Maryland:
            Newman Press.

Van der Poel, Cornelius
    1968   "The principle of double effect." Pp.186-210 in Charles Curran (ed.), *Absolutes in Moral Theology*. Washington, D.C.: Corpus Books.
Wertheimer, Roger
    1971   "Understanding the abortion argument." *Philosophy and Public Affairs* 1:67-95.
Williams, Glanville
    1957   *The Sanctity of Life and Criminal Law*. New York: Knopf.
Willson, J. Robert *et al.*
    1975   *Obstetrics and Gynecology*, 5th ed. St. Louis: C. V. Mosby Co.
Woodruff, J. Donald, and Pauerstein, Carl J.
    1969   *The Fallopian Tube: Structure, Function, Pathology, and Management*. Baltimore: Williams and Wilkins Co.
Zachery, R. B.
    1968   "Ethical and social aspects of treatment of spina bifida." *Lancet* 2:274-276.

PAPAL ADDRESSES

Pius XI
    1930   "Casti connubi." Pp. 129-140 in Raziel Abelson (ed.), *Ethics and Metaethics*. New York: St. Martin's Press, 1963.
Pius XII
    1951a   "The apostolate of the midwife." Pp. 160-176 in Vincent A. Yzermans (ed.), *The Major Addresses of Pope Pius XII*, Vol. I. St. Paul: North Central Publishing Co., 1961.
    1951b   "Morality in marriage." Pp. 185-190 in Vincent A. Yzermans (ed.), *The Unwearied Advocate: Public Addresses of Pope Pius XII*, Vol. III. St. Cloud, Minnesota: Vincent A. Yzermans, 1954.
    1957a   "Anesthesia: three moral questions: address of Pius XII to a symposium of the Italian society of anesthesiology." *The Pope Speaks* 4 (1957-8):33-49.
    1957b   "The prolongation of life: address of Pius XII to an international congress of anesthesiologists." *The Pope Speaks* 4 (1957-8):393-398.
    1958   "Morality and eugenics: address of Pius XII to the seventh international hematological congress in Rome." *The Pope Speaks* 6 (1959-60):392-400.
Paul VI
    1968   "Humanae vitae." (On the Regulation of Birth). Washington, D.C.: United States Catholic Conference.
    1972   "The right to be born." *The Pope Speaks* 17 (1972-3):333-335.

COURT CASES

    1965   *Griswold v. Connecticut*, 381 US 479.
    1972   *Byrn v. New York City Health and Hosps. Corp.*, 31 N.Y. 2d 194.
    1973   *Doe v. Bolton*, 410 US 179.
    1973   *Roe v. Wade*, 410 US 113.

INDEX